It's Good for
Your Game

Other books by Dr. T. J. Tomasi

The LAWS of the Golf Swing
(*Golf* magazine's best golf book in 1999)
(with Jim Suttie and Mike Adams)

Play Better Golf

Play Better Golf for Seniors

Play Better Golf for Women

Play Golf for Juniors

How to Break 100 in 90 Days

*Never out of the Hole:
A Player's Guide to Match Play*

How to Break 90

The Little Book of Putting

Total Golf

*The 30-Second Swing: How to Train
Your Brain to Improve Your Game*

Ask the Pro

It's Good for Your Game

Dr. T. J. Tomasi

Andrews McMeel Publishing

Kansas City

It's Good for Your Game copyright © 2003 by T. J. Tomasi. All rights reserved. Printed in the United States of America. No part of this book may be used or reproduced in any manner whatsoever without written permission except in the case of reprints in the context of reviews. For information, write Andrews McMeel Publishing, an Andrews McMeel Universal company, 4520 Main Street, Kansas City, Missouri 64111.

03 04 05 06 07   EBI   10 9 8 7 6 5 4 3 2 1

Library of Congress Cataloging-in-Publication Data

Tomasi, T. J.
    It's good for your game / T. J. Tomasi
      p. cm.
    ISBN 0-7407-1891-6
    1. Golf. I. Title.
GV965 .T625   2003
796.352—dc21
                        2002038252

Book design and composition by Kelly & Company, Lee's Summit, Missouri

——————— ATTENTION: SCHOOLS AND BUSINESSES ———————

Andrews McMeel books are available at quantity discounts with bulk purchase for educational, business, or sales promotional use. For information, please write to: Special Sales Department, Andrews McMeel Publishing, 4520 Main Street, Kansas City, Missouri 64111.

Contents

Acknowledgments

As with my previous book, *Ask the Pro,* I want to thank the team that made this book possible. Lee Salem, executive vice president at UPS, gave the go-ahead on the print side and ironed out all the details; Patrick Dobson supervised and brought the project to fruition with a nice mix of patience and dispatch. And my friend and editor, Sue Roush—the very best editor in the world—made the initial "It's Good for Your Game" readable for the *Insider Golf* page.

Introduction

*I*t's *Good for Your Game* covers the entire range of how you play golf, from learning the mechanics to some rather sophisticated nuances of the concepts that drive your body's motor behavior.

I have adapted much of the material in this book from my golf page, *Insider Golf,* which appears in newspapers and Web sites around the world. I relish the opportunity to write a weekly golf page that meets golfers of all skill ranges at the breakfast table, so to speak.

I often hear that the game is hard. Frisbee isn't hard, playing catch isn't hard, and neither are shooting hoops, fishing, or tossing a football. But most golfers will readily admit that "golf is just plain hard." It is my contention that, once you learn the mechanics of the swing, the game is not hard in and of itself. It is made hard, however, *when you ask your body to do things it can't do.* In this regard, two colleagues, Dr. Jim Suttie and Mike Adams, and I have written a book called the *The LAWs of the Golf Swing,* in which we conclude that the *way* in which golf is often taught and written about is a problem. Too often, authors of golf instruction books and teaching professionals treat every golfer the same, regardless of their physical attributes—tall and thin, short and powerful, stiff as a board, loose as a noodle. There is no question that golfers differ from one another. In conventional teaching, golfers all learn the same concept and swing mechanics. They're all asked to perform the same physical movements. It was through experimentation that Suttie, Adams, and I have come to believe that the *what* of golf-swing mechanics must change and be tailored to the individual. Golfers of different body types must use different swing mechanics.

As you might expect, my teaching is customized to the learner. In *It's Good for Your Game,* where appropriate, I have adjusted the swing vignettes contained herein to reflect this student-centered approach.

Some of the pieces of *It's Good for Your Game* overlap. The same topic presented from several vantage points is a big positive in that if one explanation doesn't quite do the trick for you, the second one no doubt will. Another advantage to our format is that because each piece is a separate entity, there is no long-term theme that must be followed, which makes this book very easy to read. You can read it all in one sitting or read it for five minutes then close it for a week. When you open it back up you won't miss a beat. And you don't have to start at the beginning—just open it anywhere and it will be, well, good for your game.

It's Good for
Your Game

■ CHAPTER 1 ■

Concepts That Are
Good for Your Game

Concept: Hit Down to Get It Up

One of the things that makes golf so difficult is that the average golfer's assumptions about how to hit good golf shots are logical but wrong. A good example is the matter of how the ball gets airborne, certainly of prime concern anywhere but on the green. Most beginners think they must lift the ball into the air by swinging upward just before impact. Unfortunately, this produces a swing that is too vertical, making it almost impossible to hit down on the ball at the correct angle. To add insult to injury, trying to lift the ball in the air encourages the weight to stay on the rear foot with the inevitable result—a golf shot that is hit thin, topped, or very fat.

Golf is a little like tiddly winks, the old game where you pressed down with the wink on the back of the tiddly to chip it into a cup. It's a matter of applying a force to the back of an object that causes it to rotate, and it's this "backspin" that creates lift. This is exactly the kind of "pinching" action that produces the backspin you need to get the ball in the air. As air flows over and under the ball at different speeds, the pressure on the top of the ball becomes lower than that underneath it, and it's this pressure differential that allows the backspin to do its job.

So in order to get the ball in the air, you must swing so the club face shaves the back of the ball through impact, creating backspin that translates into lift—and up it goes. Now the harder you hit the ball, the more spin (revolutions per second) you produce—that's why most power players hit the ball very high and weaker players hit it low.

■ *Get Groovy*

If the back of the ball is struck cleanly with a descending blow so the club face grooves are engaged, the ball will climb up the grooves, making the ball rotate backward toward the club face. The grooves create friction, which helps backspin. Technically it doesn't happen exactly this way, but the image is accurate enough to act as a good guide. Your clubs are designed with a certain amount of loft cut into the club face, ranging from perhaps 10 degrees for your driver to 60 degrees or more for your lob wedge. The more loft, the higher the ball goes, but the key is that you have to pinch the ball with your club face to take advantage of the club face loft.

Concept: The Secret of Spin

Correct spin is like money: If you have it, you don't know what all the fuss is about; when you don't have it, it's a real puzzle how other people make it happen. Here are some facts about spin that you can take to the bank: The harder you hit the ball, the more back-

The secret to imparting the correct spin to the golf ball is to have your hands ahead of the ball at impact, whether using an iron or a wood. In the photo on the left, the professional has his hands well ahead with the driver, ensuring that he will put just the right amount of backspin on the ball. When your hands are behind the ball at this point you have to flip the club face into position to make contact, and the chances of creating side spin (hooks and slices) are greatly increased. Keep the hands forward and you'll catch the irons cleanly with no gouges, because you'll take just a wisp of a divot.

spin you'll generate. That's why power players like Phil Mickelson and Tiger Woods hit the ball very high, especially with the short irons. But the closer you get to the green, the harder it is to spin the ball, because your swing speed is lower. This is why when smart players can't reach the green, they lay up to a point where they can make a full swing with a wedge, ensuring that they can hit the ball hard enough to control the ball using backspin.

Certain conditions affect backspin. For example, wet conditions decrease friction, and this reduces backspin—so you hit shots that flutter like knuckleballs. Hitting into the wind increases backspin, while playing downwind takes it off. The type of ball you use makes a big difference. The key to long drives is a low spin rate with a high launch angle—see your PGA pro for personalized advice as to which ball is right for you. Remember, it's a trade-off between distance off the tee and control around the green. The would-be 80 shooter may well prosper using a higher-spin ball (just the opposite of what most do), since the more greens you miss, the more you need control chipping and pitching.

Concept: Momentum

As kids, the closest most of us ever got to Perfect Mo was the Three Stooges (Larry, Curly, and Moe, the brains of the outfit). But there is another Perfect Mo—a force called momentum—and it can be the brains of *your* outfit when it comes to your swing. I've written before about a principle of physics called the conservation of momentum, an intimidating name for something we see every day. A graphic example: When your car is traveling at say fifty mph and you slam on the brakes, everything that's not tied down keeps going forward with a shattering force due to the momentum of the car. Momentum is termed "power in motion," and if left alone it produces "perfect motion." The point here is that most golfers do not leave Mo alone; they get involved and try to consciously make the movements happen, and that ruins the motion. To make Mo your friend when you hit a golf shot, do the following:

1 You have to set up correctly. That involves grip, stance, posture, ball position, aim, and alignment. This may sound like a lot, but it involves relatively low level skills that anyone can learn. Your movements can't be right if you start incorrectly.

2 The correct grip pressure is a little harder to do because the tendency is to squeeze the handle so tightly that Mo can't cock and uncock your wrists correctly.

3 Once your swing gets going you need to *let* things happen rather than *make* them happen. This one is tough, because when golfers want the ball to go to target, they often try to force it there with a lunge or lurch at just the wrong time—and that alienates our friend Mo.

■ What Your Friend Mo Can Do for You

If you've followed the directions above, your body will respond to momentum—your wrists will set due to Mo; your weight will shift when it should; and your right elbow will fold correctly. On the downswing, the wrists will release, the weight will shift when it should, and the right elbow will lose its bend right on time, all due to your good friend Mo.

Concept: Swing Length

During a typical round of golf you face a number of situations that require less than a full swing. You might, for example, play a low punch shot under a tree branch, make a three-quarter wedge shot, or simply take a little heat off a midiron for increased control. The problem facing you in each situation is that while you may recognize the need for a less than full swing, it's hard to know the exact length of the swing needed to execute the shot. The easiest guide for controlling the length of your swing is your target arm.

Imagine the arc of your swing as a large clock, your head at twelve o'clock and your feet at six o'clock, with your lead arm as the hour hand. For a short swing move your left arm to eight o'clock; for a half swing move it to nine o'clock; and when you want to dial in a three-quarter swing, move your target arm to ten o'clock. Your standard full swing is somewhere between ten o'clock and eleven thirty.

There are two swing keys to keep in mind as you execute these partial shots: First, be certain to turn your chest along with your target arm. Second, maintain a relaxed feeling in your wrists so the weight of the club will properly cock your wrists. This natural cocking action is the key to producing proper club-head velocity. As always, when attempting to incorporate a new element into your game, you should work out the kinks of these partial shots on the practice tee. You might even try hitting a few shots while watching your target arm as you swing. This may seem difficult at first, but that's what the practice range is for.

Concept: The Release

To give my students the concept of the release of the club head to the ball through impact, I often use this image: a horse and rider approach a six-foot wall at full gallop; suddenly the horse stops and the rider is catapulted over the wall. In your golf swing, your trunk is the horse, the wall is your front leg, the rider is your club head. The rider's abrupt separation from the horse is the release of the club head to the ball. Note that the release is "passive," a key that will allow you to create power and accuracy without trying to. Here's the concept of a good release in a nutshell: You don't *make* it happen, you *let* it happen.

If you're hitting it short and not striking the ball solidly, it may be because you don't create a wall to hit over. Most golfers simply slide their hips laterally toward the target and don't rotate them nearly enough, so there is nothing to hit against. Slide the hips without rotating them and your release will be forced and jerky,

The good player hits across the lower left leg just as the home-run hitter does. The idea is to get to your left side to start your downswing and then rotate that front hip behind you. It's just physics: slam on the breaks correctly and everything that isn't tied down (your arms, right hip, right knee, and most importantly your club head) shoots forward automatically with a powerful swinging action.

causing a mere flick of your wrists at the ball. One reason a Tour swing looks so smooth is that the release is caused by hitting the front-leg wall and not by a conscious manipulation of any part of the body.

So for a good release, firm up that front leg through impact—don't allow it to buckle or bow out toward the ball. Your front knee begins to straighten as your hip turns behind you, and while it doesn't have to go ramrod stiff, it must be firm enough to provide resistance.

Concept: Something to Nothing

■ *A Golf Swing About Nothing*

The golf swing is *something to nothing*. It's a process of getting ready—doing all the things in the same sequence to prepare for a proper impact position, and then doing nothing, letting physics do its job. You've heard it said many times that the ball only knows impact. It doesn't care how you got there, what your backswing looked like, how much money you have in the bank, or how nice a person you are; regardless of all these incidentals, the ball will instantly adopt the characteristics (expressed as spin, speed, and direction) that your club delivers to it during the collision.

One way to think of it is that the role of the setup is to arrange a collision between the club head and the ball, and there are certain things you do in your preparation, setup, and backswing that best satisfy the collision requirements. This is the "something" part of your swing, and any conscious attention is directed here.

But once you have done your "something," then you must switch off at the top of your swing and do your "nothing" the rest of the way. It's during the nothing phase that you reap the reward of your proper something. Unfortunately, doing nothing is the hardest thing for humans. Among all species we are truly the great manipulators and, while it has allowed us to rise to the top of the food chain, manipulation has also ruined many a golf swing.

Concept: Levers

Levers are part of the coiling process, because they multiply the force of your swing. Your shoulders and arms form one lever; another lever is a 90-degree angle between the lead arm and the club shaft. A third power angle comes from the same angle that you create at the elbow to throw a ball. I call it the "Power V," and it's one of the most powerful levers in the human body. When your trail arm suddenly straightens during the downswing, it ratchets up the energy delivered to the ball. These angles are absent at address, so part of the something is the formation of these levers during the backswing. The nothing part comes when these angles release on their own during the downswing.

Concept: Spine Angle

When you assume your address position, you establish the radius of your swing, which is your arm length plus your club length. Say your arm length is 32 inches with a club length of 38 inches. This gives you a swing radius of 70 inches as measured from your club head to the tip of your shoulder. To have any chance of solid contact, you must return to the ball with a radius of 70 inches.

Even though you maintain a consistent radius, you have another task. Your swing axis (your spine angle) must remain constant. This is somewhat simplistic, but close enough to make the point—if you stand up through impact you will top the ball, and if you drop into the ball, you will hit behind it, producing the dreaded fat shot. Once you know the general problem, all you need to do is the following drill that allows you to experience what it feels like to keep your body level as you swing with no dropping down and no straightening up.

Choose a short iron, and find a wall where you can make a golf swing. Take your address position with your head resting lightly against the wall. Now make a three-quarter swing using a slow and easy pace. As you swing, your head can rotate and slide a bit, but it should remain in place touching the wall until you are well into your follow-through. The point of the drill is that by maintaining the level of your head, you will retain your overall body level from the take-away through your downswing, and you will arrive at impact with the same "effective length" club as you had at address. This is the hallmark of a good swing.

Concept: To Rid Yourself of the Slice, Hook It First

There are usually two aspects of the common slice. At impact the path of the club head is traveling across the intended line of flight from the outside to the inside. And the club face is open to the intended line of flight. The result is the ball starting to the left of the target and curving severely to the right. Below is a drill that will cure your slice.

In the first part of the drill, address the ball normally and then drop your right foot back until your toe line is at approximately a 45-degree angle to your intended line of flight, as I am doing on page 11 (this is a severely "closed stance"). Notice the two boards, which are on the ground for a reference. From this stance your downswing path may be outside your backswing path but is still *inside your intended line of flight*.

Now as you approach the ball from the inside rotate your right forearm over your left to square the club face through impact. If you do this correctly your forearms will almost touch after impact with the club face looking behind you at a right angle to your intended line of flight. Using this drill you will soon be hitting powerful hooks. As you ingrain the feelings of an inside approach and a constant rate of closing, begin to square your stance until you determine where to position your right foot to ensure that your downswing path remains inside your intended line of flight. Golfers who have a chronic slice all want to hook the ball—this drill shows you how.

The antislice drill helps you feel the two opposite dynamics—an inside-to-out approach of the club head with the club face closing (turning to the left) through impact.

Concept: Hold That Angle

A good way to think of your backswing is that its role is to create certain power angles between you and your golf club that help you to multiply the force of your swing. Once you create these angles, you need to keep them intact until just before impact. One of the most important of these angles is the one created by your trail wrist as it bends into a "hinged" position at the top of your backswing. Your wrist will do this naturally in response to the momentum of your backswing if you allow it to happen.

Returning the club head to the ball is another story. During the downswing, there are strong forces pulling on the club head that can cause golfers to lose the crucial trail-wrist hinge much too early in the downswing. When this happens your swing springs a power leak and all you can do is deliver a weak slap at the ball, a mistake that kills both your distance and your accuracy.

To avoid this power loss, practice holding your trail-wrist angle in place from the top of your backswing all the way through the impact zone. You won't actually be able to accomplish this when you swing at full speed, but by trying, you should rid your swing of the "slapstick" act.

At first, keeping your wrist bent (concave) longer than you're used to will feel like you can't square the club face in time for impact. But you'll soon realize that doing so will allow you to square the club face to the ball with power, not by manipulating the club face with your hands, but through the proper rotation of your body. A

At the top of your swing let your trail wrist set so your palm faces the sky. Once you create this position keep it until just before impact. Many golfers lose the angle formed by their trail wrist too early on the forward swing. To avoid this, practice holding your right wrist angle in place all the way down to the ball.

word of caution: While you focus on keeping your trail wrist bent, make sure to allow your trail elbow to straighten naturally as you swing the club down and toward the ball.

Concept: Coil

There's no question that your hips power your golf swing, so getting just the correct amount of hip rotation is important. But I'd like to suggest that creating power is not just a question of hip rotation; rather it's how much you rotate your hips in relation to how much you rotate your chest and shoulders. This difference is called *coil*, and it is far more important than just turning.

To coil correctly you must set one part of your body against the other so that torque is produced. When you turn your shoulders more than your hips during your backswing you stretch the big, banded muscles of your back, pelvis, and thighs, and this translates into club-head speed through the impact zone.

If you turn your hips and shoulders the same amount you never produce any resistance. Here's the concept: *There's a turn in every coil but not a coil in every turn.* You may have heard that it's correct to turn your shoulders 90 degrees and your hips 45 degrees, but that varies with how you're built. If you're not very flexible and can only turn your shoulders 80 degrees, then you should try for a 40-degree hip turn. If you're super-Gumby and can turn your shoulders 100 degrees, then shoot for a hip turn of about 50 degrees or less if you can take the strain.

Actually, there is no such thing as a pure 90-degree shoulder turn because most humans can only rotate the spine (shoulders) about 35 to 45 degrees. The rest of the rotation (in this case, 45 degrees) is due to hip rotation.

The key is to develop just the right amount of hip versus shoulder turn for your physique. Flexible or not, create as large a differential as you can between your shoulders and your hips as the model on the right demonstrates.

Concept: Staying Behind the Ball

A major error occurs just before impact if you let your head slide past the ball. This is a move that delays the release of the club head to the ball and leaves your club face open, often producing a slice. This swing fault is made worse by trying to keep your head down and/or stock still. You would think that with all the bad things this shibboleth (don't move the head) has done, it would have lost its reputation by now, but I see a lot of beginners captured by it. Tests show the head floats in the good swing because, biomechanically, it has to. If it is not allowed to move you will almost always hang on your left side, a mistake that forces the club off the proper swing arc. In addition, by riveting your head too stiffly you're liable to get a pain in the neck.

In a good backswing, the head actually makes two movements; it swivels away from the target as it "floats" back toward the rear hip. And during the forward swing, the head retraces its steps as it swivels toward the target and floats back to its address position. When you allow your head to move properly during the backswing, three things should occur—you can remember them by thinking "shift, turn, and float." Shift your weight into your trail hip, turn your head along with your shoulders, and let your head move slightly away (float) from the target. This will put you in a coiled position, loaded powerfully behind the ball.

On the way down to the ball, the head returns to its original position and then, just before impact, it moves down and back away from the target in response to the release of the club. This recoil action allows the club to sling by the player at great speeds as the club face comes square to the target at impact. It's called "staying behind the ball," and it assumes that on the backswing, the player got behind the ball in the first place.

How much your head floats with your body turn depends on your body build. If you're thin, the float will be slight. Medium builds demand a bit more, and if you have a thick chest your head float will be noticeable. One caveat: While your head moves around behind the ball prior to impact, it should never move past the ball toward the target until after the ball is on its way. Actually, it's the swing center, a point just below the chin, that must stay behind the ball, but everyone uses the head, perhaps because the head has ears and the swing center does not. In any case, you can get yourself in a pickle if you slide your head past the ball, so remember— *the head floats behind the ball but never a-head of it.*

Concept: Swing Plane

The plane of your swing is established by the angle your club shaft creates with the ground at address. You'll want your club to return to impact at essentially the same angle or slant it had at address so your club face can "look" at the target as you make contact with the ball. When your club shaft matches the angle established at address throughout your backswing and downswing, it's called an "on plane swing," a very accurate way to make a golf swing.

Each club in your bag has a different shaft angle drilled into the neck of your club head, so if you carry fourteen clubs you have fourteen different slants or angles to your swing, depending on the club you're using. For example, your five-iron, assuming it's correctly soled, creates an angle with the ground of 62 degrees, while your nine-iron has a shaft angle of 66 degrees. This means that your swing with your nine-iron will be more upright or vertical than with your five-, and your five-iron much more upright than your driver (55 degrees). Thus the plane angle of each swing is established by the club you choose for the shot, and each time you change clubs, you change the angle of your swing. The nice part is that you don't have to consciously adjust your swing, because the correct progression of shaft angles is built into your clubs at the factory.

There are a lot of good players who leave the plane angle on the backswing, then return to it on the downswing, but the best way to learn the golf swing is to stay on plane from start to finish. In essence, everything you do in terms of weight shift, shoulder rotation, wrist set, and all the other in-swing mechanics is dedicated to keeping your club shaft on plane. The best way to train yourself to be on plane is as follows: Plant a shaft in the ground about three feet behind you on your toe line. Make sure it's at the exact angle of your club shaft at address (start with a seven-iron). Now take

Actually, the phrase *on-plane swing* is somewhat deceptive because it implies that there is one ideal plane (defined as an inclined straight line connecting at least two points) for each swing. In fact, there are many planes established as you swing the club but there is only one "plane angle" as established by the lie of the golf club. In geometry two parallel lines that intersect a third line form what are called congruent angles. Thus if the lie angle of your club at address is 62 degrees and during your backswing you cock your wrists so that the shaft of your club points at the ground at an angle of 62 degrees, then you are "on" the same plane angle. Your shaft angle at address and your shaft angle during backswing are parallel to each other, and both intersect the ground—thus they are congruent or *on the plane angle.* I include this for the few readers who are sticklers for terminology, but I can assure you that the ball doesn't know all this nor does it care.

some practice swings in slow motion, stopping halfway back and halfway down to check that the angles of the two shafts match. Then tee up the ball and hit some shots where your shafts match at both halfway points—halfway back and halfway down.

Concept: Learning From Your Mistakes

Some golf instructors avoid all references to the "bad," believing that if students consciously think about what they're doing wrong, they'll perform badly. Without a doubt, it is a good idea not to dwell on mistakes; however, your brain works effectively by comparing what you want your body to do with what you don't want it to do. So in order to learn how to do something correctly in your swing, it can be helpful to know what's wrong, and then do the opposite.

An example involves learning how to shift the weight properly on the backswing. It's difficult for many golfers to combine the two moves of (1) rotating the shoulders (turning the back to the target) and (2) transferring the weight to the trail hip joint. The most common pitfall is to turn the upper body without shifting the weight. This leaves the player stranded with the weight on the front side at the top of the backswing. The result is often a reverse weight shift on the downswing as the weight is shifted from the target side to the trail side—just the opposite of what it should be.

To learn how to make a new, correct weight shift, make a swing with the incorrect weight shift and tell yourself, "No, that's wrong." Then make a swing with a correct weight shift and tell yourself, "Yes, that's right." When you talk to yourself this way, you assign an "auditory tag" to an action. By telling yourself that something is wrong, you label that action off limits. Conversely, by telling yourself that something is right, you label that action as worth repeating.

So the next time you identify an error in your golf swing, don't try to forget it immediately. Instead, use the faulty move to help ingrain the proper move—*then* forget it.

Concept: Mental Imagery

The number one rule is that you "work" (draw, fade high and low) the ball with your setup and your follow-through—not by manipulating your golf swing. But don't forget to imagine your shot. Your mind is very powerful, so how you "see" your swing influences how you actually execute it. Images cue motor behavior, and the more vivid and complete your image is, the more precise the cue. Great players use imagery for every shot. Chi Chi Rodriguez, a premier shot maker, explains that he "paints the portrait" of every shot in his mind before he hits it. Sam Snead, when asked how he curves the ball, said, "I just think fade or draw." Jack Nicklaus claims that he "goes to the movies" before every shot and sees the shot exactly as it should be before he makes the actual swing. Seve Ballesteros and Greg Norman do much the same, as do most good players.

Concept: The Importance of the Follow-Through

While it's important to imagine your swing as a whole (see it, feel it, and even hear it), pay special attention to your *follow-through*. While you never consciously try to curve the shot with your swing (that's overmanipulation), you do want to have a very clear concept in your mind of your finish position before you swing. For the draw finish your club shaft tilts (club head first) to the left of target; for the fade it tilts to the right. When you want a high shot imagine a high finish, while to keep your shot low, imagine a low finish.

Jack Nicklaus finishes with the shaft tilted to the right, ensuring that the ball will spin from left to right.

If you want to draw the ball, set up for a draw and program your mind that your swing is on the way to a draw finish. Then, free from any in-swing manipulations, let your golf swing benefit from the geometry you established at address between your body, club, the ball, and your target. Once this is done, simply swing through to the appropriate finish position. The same holds true for the other specialty shots, including the fade, the high shot, and the low shot.

Concept: Elbow Even or in Front of the Hip

When you watch a well-blended swing it looks like the arms simply follow the body as it turns. But the eye is deceived because that's not what happens. It's a basic tenet of my teaching that the arms do the up-and-down and the body does the around, and they must not get into each other's business.

Here I focus on the mistake where the arms horn in on the business of the body (the "around business"), trapping the club head behind you. This happens during the backswing when the body turns and the arms simply follow the body, swinging the club much too far in back of you. At the top of your swing, if your back elbow is too far behind you it takes too long for it to get even (or slightly in front) of your hip, where it should be during your downswing. The elbow trapped behind the hip results in the faulty downswing position where the elbow is *still* behind the hip near impact. From here you have to do something funny like flip your hands to save the shot, and that's not good.

In the correct downswing, the elbow position is pointed toward the ground and more in line with the right hip. There are not many nonnegotiables in this game—things that everyone must do when swinging a golf club—but the proper elbow position is one of them, because it allows your arms to get back in front of your body and square the club face at impact. When you look at the very best swings, you'll always see the trailing forearm even with the hip and "looking" at the sky in the latter part of the downswing.

Concept: Arms and Body Together

Your arms dictate the speed of the swing, and your hands and forearms time the release of the club through impact. There's a noticeable rotation of the forearms that, coupled with the uncocking of the wrists, allows the toe of the club to rotate past the heel through the hitting zone. This is an antislice action that can produce anything from a straight shot to a duck hook, depending on the amount and timing of your forearm rotation.

When your timing is good, you'll be rewarded with generally accurate shots. However, if your timing is less than perfect, you'll be in for a long round filled with crooked shots. Without a doubt it's in your best interest as a player to learn how to generate a perfect blend of arm and chest rotation that squares the club face to the ball at impact. The problem is that on the golf course, it's all too easy to get anxious from the top of the swing and spin your chest or overuse your hands and arms. The more you play and practice, the easier it will be to find the correct blend between arms and body.

A good drill that will help you find a happy medium is to tee the ball and hit seven-irons with your legs so close together that the insides of your ankles are touching. Your goal is to hit the ball about 50 yards with a slight draw. This drill will teach you to blend your chest rotation with your arm rotation. Concentrate on releasing the club with a soft but constant rotation of your forearms during the downswing. Don't hold your chest back but let its turn be paced by your arm swing. When you do it correctly you'll feel as if your arms are swinging past the midline of your body; it's the momentum generated by that action that pulls your chest around.

Concept: The Role of the Ankle Roll

One of the first to emphasize the importance of the ankles in the golf swing was Alex Morrison. A pupil of his, Jack Grout, passed the information to a fairly decent player, one Jack Nicklaus, whose swing for many years served as a clinic for demonstrating perfect ankle action.

The ankle is a hinge joint, whose range of motion includes allowing the leg to move inward toward the center of the body while the foot remains essentially in place. This rolling motion, while possible, is rarely used. Much more common is lifting the heel and the knee

Senior Tour star Tom Wargo demonstrates the ankle roll through impact. The left ankle rolls inward in a similar fashion during the backswing. Basically you play this game on the inner rims of your feet with everything turning in toward the center line of your body.

together, a habit ingrained from walking. Because it's so natural, many golfers simply lift their front heel and knee straight up during the backswing, thus ruining their weight shift. During the downswing they make the same mistake with the back heel, leaving most of their weight on the trail side.

If you're hitting a lot of fat shots and the best thing you can say about your overall pattern of shots is that it's erratic, check to see if you're performing the ankle roll.

■ How to Roll Your Ankles

Done correctly, the ankle roll allows you to keep your body level while you rotate around your hip joints as you swing. On the backswing, your front ankle (right) folds inward toward the center line of your body in response to the pull of your front knee as it moves behind the ball. The amount it rolls depends on your flexibility— the outside of your front foot may leave the ground as your weight shifts into your back hip joint, especially with the longer clubs like the driver. But even though your front heel leaves the ground, your front knee and ankle should not move vertically upward. During your downswing your trailing angle rolls inward, onto its inner rim, following the lead of your back knee and hip as they fire target ward.

A good check point is to examine the top of your golf shoes as the start of both your backswing and downswing. Either use video with a zoom, or ask a friend to watch for the appearance of wrinkles across the top of your shoes where your toes meet your foot. Wrinkles indicate that you're lifting your heel rather than rolling your ankle.

Concept: Dancing With the One You Brought

■ *The Alternate Target Method*

There are two ways you can cope with a slice or hook that develops out on the course. The correct method gets you through a round quite nicely, while the wrong method can multiply your problems and run up your score.

The less seasoned golfer who develops a slice during the round makes it progressively worse as follows: You hit one slice and you open your stance, trying to aim left of the target to play for the next slice. The more you open your body, the more you cut across the ball, so subconsciously you aim even more left. The more your ball slices the more you aim left, and the more you aim left, the more you must leave the club face open, producing bigger and bigger slices. Unfortunately there aren't many golf holes you can play aiming 80 yards left of the target, especially if the wind is blowing.

The more experienced player knows how to get the ball around the golf course even when he feels he's "lost" his swing. You can manage your bad days like a Tour player by following this procedure. Standing behind the ball, identify your primary target (the flag) and then choose an alternate target, like a tree or a bunker you can't reach. For example, if you're slicing your ball about 20 yards off line, pick an alternate target 20 yards to the left of your real target. Aim your club face to the alternate target and align your body square to your alternate target line. Then make the same swing you've been making all day, letting the ball curve back to your primary target.

Though it's not much fun struggling with your swing for eighteen holes, learning to manage a slice or a hook on the course is a satisfying example of self-control and it will show up in your scores. It's estimated that you have your A swing only 10 percent of the time, so to be a good player you have to learn to get the ball in the hole no matter what swing you've got that day. The key to consistent scoring is the ability to make the best of the worst.

■ CHAPTER 2 ■

Preswing Swing Mechanics

The Grip

■ *Placement of the Target Hand*

One of the key elements of a good grip is how you place your target hand (the left for right-handers) on the club. Remember that once your club starts down from the top of your swing, its speed increases substantially. Thus it's essential that you anchor the club securely at address so that it's under your control while you swing. As Tommy Bolt said, to be a player you've got to "own" the club, and if it's sliding around in your hand, it owns you.

To position your target hand correctly, extend your arms and hold the club at a 90-degree angle in front of you with the heel pad of your target hand on top of the handle. This places the club across the top joints of the fingers (where the fingers meet the hand). The club rests against your knuckle joints so that when you close your hand, the club is anchored under the heel pad, giving you control of the club without creating arm tension. Since the heel pad secures

For maximum control, use a medium-long thumb—halfway between full extension and complete retraction. Place your thumb down the backside of the shaft so that your wrist joint is directly on top of the club handle. This is important because if it is done correctly, the joints of your shoulder, elbow, and wrist line up with the club face at impact to give accurate golf shots.

the club, you don't have to squeeze the club to death to control it, and it is this lack of tension that allows your wrist to hinge properly during your backswing.

Unfortunately, most golfers who set the club head behind the ball and then take their grip often get the club too diagonal in their hand—too much in the palm of the hand—making it difficult to cock their wrists. By placing the grip under the heel pad, you not only anchor the club, but during your backswing you make it easier to create the 90-degree angle between your target arm and the club shaft, the important lever that gives you power.

One last thing: When placing your target hand on the club, ignore the markings on the grip—they are not meant as guides for your hands.

The club is anchored securely under the fat pad of the hand. Ignore the standard instruction to increase the pressure in the last three fingers of your left hand. The only pressure point you need is where the right fat pad of the thumb presses down on the top joint of your left thumb. To get the feeling, place a tee under your right thumb and hit a few practice balls.

■ Placement of the Trail Hand

While gripping the club with your left hand as outlined above (your left arm is still extended in front of you), place the middle segments of your two middle fingers on the underside of the grip so they lightly contact your left index finger. Now close your right palm over your left thumb. Your right index finger wraps around the club, very close to your middle finger. Last, let your pinkie finger fall into place approximately over the ridge between your left index and middle finger.

■ End the Hand-to-Hand Combat: Unitize Your Grip

Your hands must be placed on the club so they're not fighting one another for control. I've described the overlap grip, but it doesn't matter much if you overlap, baseball it, or interlock, because your brain doesn't care and neither does the ball. What your brain does care about is feel, or more exactly, pressure. Your hands are the tactile center of everything you do, including swinging a golf club. Your hands interpret the world—they're ultrasensitive pressure gauges—

To unitize your hands there is only one pressure point necessary, and that's where the right fat pad of the thumb presses down on the top joint of your left thumb.

and if you don't believe it, try wearing thick gloves for an hour and you'll feel what I mean. There's another part of this hands thing that's important: You've got two of them and they work very well together on many of the special assignments you give them, like covering both ears when the boss hollers at you or holding on for dear life to the new Ming vase you just bought as you carry it home.

But sometimes your hands fight one another for control, a civil war, left against right. This is disruptive especially during your downswing, with the left trying to pull, and the right wanting to push. Unfortunately, it doesn't matter which hand wins because you lose. Thus the basic fundamental of your grip is to hold the club in such a way that the brain interprets your hands as a unit, a clamp, not for crushing but for control.

To unitize your hands, you need only one pressure point, and that's where the fat pad of your right thumb presses down on the top

WHAT TO DO WITH THE PINKIE

What should you do with the little finger of your lower hand when you take hold of the club? It's your choice. There are three common ways to hold the club: the first is called the overlapping grip, or the Vardon grip, where your right pinkie (for right-handers) sits on top of your left index finger. Its called the Vardon grip because it was popularized (although he didn't invent it) by the great English player Harry Vardon.

The second option for your pinkie is known as the interlocking grip. With this grip, the right pinkie intertwines around the left index finger with the tip of the right pinkie nearly touching the knuckle on the left index finger. This is the method used by many great players (including Jack Nicklaus and Tiger Woods) who began playing as young kids. This is the best way to anchor the club given the weak hands of a child.

The third way you can arrange your fingers is called the ten-fingered grip, where the fingers neither intertwine nor overlap but simply rest against one another with a very light pressure. This type of grip is sometimes called the baseball grip because it resembles how you hold a baseball bat, except that your thumbs are pointing down the handle of the club instead of wrapping around a bat.

Basically how you relate the index finger of your bottom hand and the pinkie of your top hand is a matter of personal preference. I recommend that you choose the grip that feels best for you and then see your PGA pro to make sure it's correct.

Here I demonstrate the least common of the three most typical ways of holding the club. The baseball grip allows no intertwine or overlap of the little finger.

joint of your left thumb. Not only does it press down as you take your grip, but you should squeeze it (milk it a tad) so it lies directly over the entire left thumb. This unitizing pressure point ends the tug of war.

■ *The Strong Grip/Weak Grip Dilemma*

The strong grip is present when the Vs formed by the thumb and forefinger of each hand point toward the back shoulder, a grip currently favored by such players as Fred Couples, Paul Azinger, and David Duval. In the weak grip (e.g., Jose Maria Olazabal's), the Vs point at the nose or even to the target-side cheek. In the neutral grip used by the majority of Tour players, the Vs point somewhere between the back shoulder and the chin.

Explaining the strong grip in terms of where the Vs formed by your thumb and forefinger are pointing is a useful guide that suggests how aggressively your club face responds to the release through the impact zone. Unless other elements of your swing prevent it, the rule of thumb is that the more your hands are rotated away from the target at address as you take hold of the club, the stronger the grip and the more your club face closes during contact, producing a draw or, if the club face turns over too much, a hook.

The opposite can be said of the weak grip, where the hands are rotated toward the target, causing less turnover and usually producing a fade or a slice. This is not always the case, especially with Tour players, many of whom fade the ball from a strong grip or draw with a weak grip. But the distinction (strong grip = draw or hook, weak grip = fade or slice) normally applies for the average amateur golfer.

The aforementioned "rule of thumb" is a bit more important than it might first appear, for the target thumb (the thumb of the highest hand of your grip) plays a major role in the rotation of the club face through impact.

■ Thumb Positioning

The position of your target thumb on the club handle determines the direction in which force is applied to the shaft during your release and, therefore, how much the face of your club face will rotate through the impact. When your thumb is on the top of the shaft at address, the pressure it exerts during your release is down the middle of the club shaft, reducing club-face rotation. This means that unless there is a compensation, you'll hit a fade or a slice. With your target thumb down the back of the shaft, a force is applied that causes your club face to rotate aggressively through impact, imparting the characteristic right to left spin of the draw shot.

Finding just the right grip for you strength-wise is a matter of experimentation, and no grip is intrinsically better than another, although the modern tendency on the Tour is toward the stronger grip. Where on the continuum of grip strength you fall depends on the type of ball flight you want and how the grip fits in with the rest of the facets of your swing. In general, if you are a slicer you should make your grip stronger and if you're a hooker, make it weaker.

■ Long or Short Thumb

You may never have thought about it, but when you grip the golf club with your top hand you can position your thumb several ways. You can extend it as far as it will go so it lays flat on the grip in what is known as the "long thumb" position; retract it up the grip as far as possible into the position known as the "short thumb"; or adjust to a position in between the short and the long. The long thumb gives your wrists the most range of motion, allowing you to make the largest wrist cock possible, and that translates into a long swing arc. The short thumb cuts down on your wrist's range of motion, reducing the length of your swing arc, a plus for control if you're prone to overswinging. The middle position is the compromise option that is most common with good players.

Aim and Alignment

Golfers are sometimes confused by the terms *square, open,* and *closed,* and that's understandable. After all, the phrase *open stance* means the body is pointing to the left of the target at address, while an *open club face* at address describes a club face that points right of the target. To clear up the confusion, let's start with the term *square.*

When the club face is square at address, it is pointed directly down the target line, so that its leading edge is *perpendicular* to the target

YOUR BODY DICTATES

If you're a golfer with a large chest and limited flexibility, try a stronger grip position—that is, rotate your lead hand clockwise until it's more on top of the handle. This combined with a neutral trail-hand grip position (palm facing target) helps you to cock your wrists and create extension in your backswing by swinging the club head in a wide arc—something your body characteristics make difficult to do.

line. If your address position is square, your body (feet, hips, and shoulders) are positioned *parallel* to the target line.

To help get a more concrete idea of what the terms mean, lay four clubs down on the ground in the form of a square, with one club laying directly on the target line. These clubs will clearly illustrate the geometric relationship between your body, the club face, and the target line. Position a ball in the upper right-hand corner outside the square and assume a square address position, with your body lines parallel to the club lying on the target line. Make sure that your club face is also square, that is, positioned perpendicular to the shaft representing the target line. You can now understand why the terms *open, closed,* and *square* mean different things for body alignment and club face aim: For the former your body is positioned parallel to the target line, while for the latter your club face sets up perpendicular to it—a very significant difference. This is why a stance in which a *club face* is pointing to the right of the target line is termed "open," while you are said to have a "closed" stance if your *body* points to the right of the target line.

Now to open your stance, simply draw your front foot back from its square position so that your toe line is now diagonal to the target line instead of parallel. To close it, draw your back foot away from square. To "square up" again, adjust your feet so the toe line is parallel with the target line.

■ Aim, Then Align

Whatever else golf is, it's a game of geometry—lines and angles on a four-dimensional playing field that relate the golfer, the ball, and the target. The mistake I see most in my teaching is a faulty setup, which is like beginning your trip by heading in the wrong direction. The first step to a perfect setup is to aim your club face correctly, while the second is to align your body. So the sequence is *aim, then align.*

■ Aiming

It seems an easy task: Just aim the club face at the target. However, it's not quite as simple as that, because not only is the target for a full swing a long way away but, by the rules of golf, you're mandated to stand to the side of the ball, an awkward position for aiming unless you know what you're doing. Unfortunately, some golfers are either too embarrassed to ask how to point the club face, or, more likely, they don't know they're misaiming; so they play for years with the wrong idea of what their club face should look like sitting there behind the ball.

The problem is that a poorly aimed club face encourages swing errors. I routinely see students with a closed club face at address, the signature of a golfer trying to stop the slice. This compensation is a particularly dangerous one, because sometimes it works and sometimes it doesn't, so you can never be sure what kind of shot you're going to hit. If you're a slicer, but several times a round you

It's helpful to use the lines on the toe and heel formed by the grooves on your club face for aiming. Take great care to aim your club face at the target at address because that's where you want it looking at impact.

hit a big pull or a pull hook, you may well have a closed club face at address.

Not as common, but just as debilitating, is the hooker, who opens the club face to stop those dreaded right-to-left snappers. In any case if you're playing with either an open or closed club face at address, learning the fundamentals of a square face will allow you to prune your golf swing of those nasty compensating errors.

■ About Your Face

First, some basics about your club face: At address, the toe of your club head is the part farthest from you and the heel of the club is the part closest to you. The *hosel* is the protrusion above the heel where the shaft is connected to the club face. The horizontal lines on your club face are called *grooves,* and the vertical lines formed by the ends of each groove on the toe and heel are what I call the *aiming lines.*

A Square Face

Your club face is square when the leading edge on the bottom of your club face is perpendicular to your target line so that the aiming lines face directly at the target. When your face is square, the toe is slightly behind the heel as the club rests behind the ball. Aiming lines that look left of the target occur when your club face is closed with the toe turned in toward your toe line. An open face occurs when the heel is turned out toward the target line, causing the aiming lines to point to the right of target.

It's helpful to use the lines on the toe and heel formed by the grooves on your club face for aiming. It may sound simplistic, but you must take great care to aim your club face at the target at address because that's where you want it looking at impact. Always set the club face behind the ball before you take the rest of your setup, then build your stance around your club face, so that if you extended a line from the leading edge (the bottom part of the club face) to your toe line, the two lines would be perpendicular.

■ *Aligning*

Because your shoulders determine the direction your arms swing, they must be aligned correctly to ensure that your club face looks at the target at impact. Your shoulders should be parallel to the target line because your arms swing in the direction that your shoulders point. When you're aimed to the right, if you make a good swing, your swing path is too much in-to-out. The reverse is true when your stance is open.

The alignment of your hips is important because your hips dictate the amount of rotation away from and back to the ball. Open hips cause you to underturn on the backswing and therefore are too open at impact. If your hips are closed at address, you run the risk of overturning on the backswing and then not being able to get your hips turned back in time for impact.

To make sure your aim and alignment are correct, lay down two clubs—one along your foot line parallel to the target line and one behind the ball on the target line. When your body is parallel with the target line, it's said to be *square* to the target. When your club face points at the target, it is also square. Begin from a perfectly square stance and then make adjustments based on your flexibility and body shape.

■ Use an Intermediate Target

Stand behind the ball to pick your target and then choose a distinguishable mark or object on your intended target line a foot or two in front of the ball. When you walk in to address the ball, this intermediate target will help you aim your club face. Think of it this way: It's easier to line up a target that's a foot away versus one that's 150 yards.

■ Stance Width

Like many things in golf, the width of your stance (how far apart your heels are) is negotiable, which is my term to represent swing mechanics that change from player to player. But while no one stance width is right for all players, you should follow some guidelines.

Too wide a stance limits your ability to turn your hips correctly and encourages excessive lateral motion. It is a major cause of sliding ahead of the ball during the downswing, a mistake that produces, among other things, weak slices and pop-ups. Too wide a stance also makes it difficult to get behind the ball during your backswing, an error that prevents you from making a good turn away from the ball. Players with excessively wide stances are thereby prone to picking the club up to the top of the swing with little if any coiling of the body, and this leads to a weak, lunging swing lacking both grace and power.

It's somewhat paradoxical that even though a very wide stance gives you a feeling of power, the exact opposite is true when it crosses the borderline to *too* wide—too wide means too little power.

Too narrow a stance is no bargain either, because its legacy is often the dreaded reverse weight shift, where your weight stays in your front hip on the way back and then, as the club head swings to the ball on the downswing, the weight shifts into the *back* hip, just the reverse of where it should be. The correct stance width will allow the following: when the club head is moving away from the ball your weight should be on your back or trail hip; when the club head is coming toward the ball, your weight should be on your front or target hip.

You can check your stance width by addressing the ball, then turning into your follow-through position; if your knees almost touch other, your stance is the correct width. If your knees can't reach each other, your stance is too wide. If they overlap, your stance is too narrow.

■ *How to Find* Your *Perfect Knee Flex*

Notice the word *your* in the head above. It's there for a reason—the amount of knee flex you have at address is determined in large part by *your* physique and your balance system and not by some arbitrary, one-size-fits-all standard. Greg Norman, for example, bends his knees a lot at address, while Fred Couples barely bends his at all, so it's obvious that golfers can play well at both ends of the knee-bend continuum. Creating just the right amount of knee flex is important if you want to make good contact with the ball at impact.

Tiger's knees are almost touching at the finish, showing that his stance is just the right width for his golf swing.

Because the golf ball is at foot level at address, you need to do two things in order to lower your club head to the ball: bend from your hip joints and flex your knees. But too many golfers either bend their knees without bending from their hip joints or they bend from their hip joints correctly, but keep the legs straight—and I don't think you should play any sport stiff-legged. If your legs are too stiff you'll make a weak, upper-body slap at the ball. If there's too much knee flex, you're sure to come up and out of the shot. Here is how you can find your ideal knee flex.

Rather than copy an arbitrary standard or a particular Tour player, my suggestion is that you personalize your knee flex. To find your natural balance point for knee flex take your normal stride, allowing the right heel to raise off the ground as you plant your left foot flat on the ground. Stop at this point and check the amount of bend in your left knee. This is your optimum balance position, the one you automatically go to with each step you take. Now bring your right leg parallel to your left and match the amount of flex in your left knee. All you have left to do is to bend from your hip joints and stick your fanny out and you're in *your* perfect knee-flex position.

Posture

When you swing a golf club, forces are exerted on your body that can cause you to lose your balance. To withstand these forces at high speeds (long hitters swing the club head over 120 miles per hour), you must be in perfect balance, both before and during your swing. To establish proper balance at address, it's important to stick your fanny up and out behind you, as in photo (c). As your swing reaches maximum speed, your posterior acts as an anchor, which allows your arms to swing at full force on a constant arc.

As you assume the address position, imagine that you are about to sit on a high bar stool, and make sure that your rump is well behind your heels. In addition to better balance, you will gain the added benefit of a correctly angled spine, which gives you a true axis to swing around.

When you are in the proper position, you are in the same posture that all great athletes assume for action—a quarterback waiting for a snap, a basketball player preparing for a free throw, a shortstop ready for a grounder, and so on. The muscles of your thighs are taut but not tense, and if you needed to leap forward without repositioning your weight, you could.

But simply setting your derriere in the correct position is not enough. For proper dynamic balance you must also create proper weight distribution from the balls of both feet back along the arch and through to the heel with the majority located between the ball and arch. Your weight is on the inner rim of both feet with the

Most players are unbalanced at address and this translates to imbalance during the swing. For some golfers it feels powerful to bend over and reach for the ball, but this places too much weight on the toes (a). As soon as the swing starts, your weight will rock back to your heels, forcing your body to straighten up. For others it feels "safe" to stand hunched over very close to the ball with the stomach tucked in, but from this setup your body is immobilized and all you can do is deliver a weak slap to the ball (b). Both of these postures create mis-hits, especially slices and fat and topped shots. Photo (c) shows the correct posture.

With straight knees, place a shaft across your hips, parallel to the ground. Now push the shaft backward until your fanny protrudes and your weight moves to your toes. Then flex your knees until your weight is redistributed from the balls of your feet back to your heels.

knees slightly inclined inward (knock-kneed). This gives an inward thrust to the forces that provide maximum stabilization.

■ Unlock Your Hips, Unleash Your Potential

In every good golf swing, an event occurs in the transition from backswing to downswing called the *hip switch*. This is a movement in which weight transfers from the rear hip (which is the rotational center of your backswing) to the target hip, making it the rotational center for your release. This can only occur if you "unlock" the hips prior to beginning your swing by bending from the hip joints rather than from the waist. But it's not enough to just assume the position; you must be strong enough to maintain this posture throughout your swing. If you lose your posture during your swing, you'll get "locked up" and be forced to slide instead of turn.

A reminder: when you assume the correct position, your abdomen is retracted away from the ball, causing your fanny to protrude. This is the dynamic balance position where your head and shoulders pull you toward the ball as you swing, but your backside provides the counterweight to keep you in balance.

■ Bending from the Hips

Your body is designed to bend forward from the hips, not the waist. When you bend from your waist you hunch your back and deactivate your centers of rotation. For every one degree of hunch you lose two degrees of spine rotation. This is why you're often advised to try to touch your shoulder blades at address. Bending from the waist locks your hip joints, forcing your hips to move laterally, producing a slide instead of a turn. By bending from your hip joints, your arms will hang, tension free, directly below your shoulders. It will also create room for your arms to swing on the correct swing plane.

■ Shoulders

Your arms should be hanging straight down from your shoulders, with your upper arms adhering lightly to your chest as if they were

Andy Pruitt of the Boulder Center for Sports Medicine in Colorado uses this simple exercise to treat people with sore lower backs and to help them find and maintain proper golf posture: Begin by standing up straight and holding a golf club against your spine. With your knees slightly bent, and your feet about hip-width apart, bend forward from the hip sockets, maintaining the golf-club contact against your spine. Repeat several times, until you feel that your muscles have been thoroughly exercised (you should feel a slight burning sensation in the area—never outright pain).

Finally, assume your address position, emulating the feeling you developed during your exercise. Your hips are now unlocked, and you are ready to swing.

strapped on top of your chest. You're in the correct position when you can drop the club at address, relax your arms, and your arms don't change their angle of hang.

■ *Head Posture*

Your head should be positioned in the middle of your shoulders with your chin held high in the proud position. If your chin rests on your chest, it blocks your shoulder turn. The proud position requires you to "peep" at the ball from the bottom of your eyes rather than stare at it with a droopy head. Note: If you can avoid it, don't wear bifocals when you play golf, because they force you to drop your head to see the ball.

■ *Knee Flex*

As I have said, your knees are designed to bend your body backward, and as I outlined above, your knee flex should match the knee bend of your normal walking stride just as your forward foot flattens on the ground. This is your natural balance flex point, and it differs from golfer to golfer depending on flexibility and body physique. The amount of knee flex at address is also related to the length of your arms. With proper posture, golfers with short arms require more knee flex than those with longer arms. But no matter how much knee flex you have, make sure that your weight is evenly spread from the balls of your feet to your heels—never on your toes.

■ *Weight Distribution*

Staying in good balance while you swing is a fundamental, so the standard advice is to place the majority of your weight on the balls of your feet. This way you won't tilt forward toward the ball as you

At address your golf club weighs only a few ounces, but during the downswing it can have an effective weight of thirty pounds— more than enough to pull you off balance if you're not positioned correctly. With the weight on the balls of the feet you can stay balanced during your backswing, but as soon as you start the downswing the tendency is for the weight to move even more toward the toes, and in some cases this can pull the heels off the ground. To develop the feeling of the correct weight distribution at address and throughout the swing, place a shaft under the balls of your feet—this will keep from pitching forward during your downswing.

start your backswing and you'll be able to turn around the fixed axis of your spine without dipping forward toward the ball. Actually, this advice is somewhat misleading because if you put your weight on the balls of your feet you'll have it too far out on your toes. The ball of your foot is the rounded part of the bone at the base of your big toe, and you don't want your weight there.

Anatomically, it's the heavy-duty Talus bone in the arch of your foot that conducts the weight of the body into your feet. It helps connect your foot to your leg, and your weight at address should run down your lower leg, through the Talus, directly into the arch of your foot. In this position you create the stable channels of balance necessary to keep the rotary motion of your golf swing in good order.

To make sure you distribute your weight correctly, simply curl your toes at address and keep them curled as you swing. At first it may feel as if you're rocking backward as you near the top of your swing, but that's just because you're used to being too much on your toes. If you really have trouble keeping your toes curled, place an old golf shaft under the balls of your feet. This will activate your golfing "talisman" and bring you more than just luck—-it will bring your better golf balance.

Ball Position

Coiling behind the ball is necessary for power, but too many golfers play the ball so far forward they unconsciously train themselves not to coil because it feels like a sway. Another problem occurs when the golf ball is too far forward in your stance—you'll have to turn your chest toward the target in order to sole the club head directly behind the ball. This "opens" your shoulders and, because the club swings along the line of the shoulders, you're stuck with an out-to-in slicer's swing path right from the get-go.

If you're a slicer or puller of the ball with limited flexibility and/or a large chest, I recommend that you experiment playing the ball back of the standard position. (Note: In addition to moving the ball back, close your stance and flare your back foot—exactly how much you'll figure out through practice.)

Playing the ball back in your stance encourages you to coil behind the ball during your backswing because you can see when you fail to get behind it.

■ *Body Builds and Ball Position*

There are three basic body builds related to ball position: Thin chest, medium-size chest, and very large chest. Usually, but not always. thin-chested golfers have the most flexibility, large-chested golfers the least, and medium somewhere in between. These are very broad-

Think of it this way—divide your clubs into three clusters: five through sand wedge; long irons and fairway woods; and driver. If you're a thick-chested player, for medium to short irons, play the ball in the center of your stance. For long irons (which I hope you don't carry) and utility woods (which I hope you do), position the ball about one ball's width forward of the center of your stance, approximately off your cheek; for the driver and other woods off a tee, the position is two balls' width forward off your shirt logo. If your chest is moderate to small, move the ball up for all the categories by two inches.

base distinctions that depend on experimentation and customization but they do give golfers a starting point in the search for the correct ball position.

■ Medium Chest Size

For medium-chested players, the following ball positions apply. For the six-iron through the sand wedge, position the ball off your left cheek. When you're playing a long iron (1, 2, 3, 4, 5) or fairway wood, move the ball about one ball's width farther forward between your left cheek and underarm, or the logo on your shirt. For your driver, or other woods on a tee, it's off your underarm.

■ *Thin Chest Size*

Thin-chested players should experiment using the following three ball positions. For the mid- to short irons, position the ball in the middle of the left half of your chest, off the logo of your shirt. For long irons and fairway woods, position the ball in line with your left underarm, opposite your left heel. For the driver and other woods off a tee, play the ball off the tip of your left shoulder. As the ball moves forward in your stance, it must also be positioned *along the path* or curve of the swing rather than the target line. If you just move the ball forward along the target line, by the time your club head reaches the ball it will be moving inside the line and you'll hit the ball on the toe of the club. Therefore, when you position the ball forward for your teed woods, remember to move the ball *closer* to you.

■ *Large Chest Size*

The ball must be farther back in your stance than for the other body builds. Be careful to adjust your body for the correct ball position because, when the ball is back in your stance, the tendency is to aim to the right of the target. For short and medium irons, position the ball in the center of your stance, opposite your nose. Playing the ball a bit farther back than standard accommodates your strong left-hand grip, flatish shoulder turn, and closed body alignment. With long irons and fairway woods, move the ball slightly forward of center about a ball's width, opposite your left cheek. For your driver and other woods off a tee, position the ball opposite the center of the left side of your chest, where the logo on your shirt would be. The more flexible you are and the smaller your chest, the less you should close your stance. This means that your ball position will move farther forward than the prototype suggests.

■ *Make Sure Your Routine Is Routine*

A good preshot routine is an important part of shot making, something the good players have known about and been doing since golf began. Now to create a routine, you have to do the same things in the same sequence for every swing. Unfortunately, most golfers don't do this. Sometimes they stand behind the ball to plan the shot, and sometimes they just walk in from wherever they happen to be standing. One time they'll take two practice swings, another time, one, and sometimes none at all. Most of the time they take their address position by planting their feet in place first and then try to aim the club face at the target. The point is that *inconsistency in the preshot routine breeds inconsistent golf shots*. So let's get consistent.

■ *What to Do*

In order to avoid this problem, stand behind the ball and pick a specific target for every shot you hit. Take a practice swing and make it a true rehearsal of the actual shot by swinging in the direction of the target, off a similar lie, and at the same speed as the swing you are about to make. If you're hitting a driver from the tee, make sure you don't take a divot; if you're hitting an iron make sure the club takes a little grass. Once you've pictured the shot in your mind and made a practice swing, take a deep breath to relax.

Now you're ready to step into your address position with your back foot leading the way. Before you bring your front foot into position, sole the club face behind the ball, so that it points at the target. Then, keeping the club head in its exact position, bring your front foot into position so that your body is perpendicular to the leading edge of the club face. You have now locked in your direction.

From this position, take one look at the target by rotating your head without lifting it, waggle, and make your swing, allowing the speed of your swing to produce the correct distance. Each individual will incorporate nuances into the routine. For instance, you may want to look at the target twice before you swing. But the important point is to be consistent. If you normally look at the target twice, but while playing a particular shot (usually under extra pressure) you find yourself looking a third or fourth time, your routine has been broken and this is a clear indication that you're uncertain about some element of the shot. Treat this as a signal to step away, gather more information (perhaps switch clubs), and then step up to the ball with a reaffirmed commitment to your plan and make your best swing.

For more on how to maintain your composure with a perfect routine, see my book *The Thirty-Second Swing: How to Train Your Brain to Improve Your Game.*

CHAPTER 3

General Swing Mechanics

The Takeaway

Your first motion (the takeaway) is critical. A mistake here will cause other errors in your backswing and force you to try to make compensations in your downswing. A common error at this point is to lift the club head immediately as you start back with little or no shoulder movement. This gets the club off track so early in the swing that a solid hit is almost impossible.

Another problem occurs when you roll your hands and forearms, aiming the butt of the club to the right of the target by the end of the takeaway. This forces you to lift the club to reach the top of the backswing, destroying your coil and the path of your swing.

In photo (a) our model has completed a perfect takeaway by continuing to move his shoulders, hands, and arms together until the club is parallel to his stance line. Also, at this point notice that his hands are above the level of the club head. From here he's poised to complete his weight transfer and shoulder turn to a coiled position at the top (b) of the backswing.

Practice your takeaway by mimicking the positions in the two photos. A good takeaway gives you a chance to complete an efficient swing, while a bad takeaway sets up a chain reaction of errors that can only lead to inconsistency.

■ Being Well Connected

At address rest your target arm on top of your chest. The goal during the swing is to maintain this arm-to-chest connection. I see many golfers who lose this contact during the backswing, and this makes it very difficult to return the club face correctly at impact. To feel the connection, place a headcover under your target arm, then keep it there with light pressure all the way to the top of your swing and well into your follow-through until your connection is naturally broken as your arms raise above your shoulders and the headcover falls to the ground.

Your target arm is an important part of the radius of your swing and it controls the position of your club face. If you keep your radius intact from setup to impact your ball striking will be very consistent. Unfortunately most golfers change the radius as they swing and are forced to make some sort of adjustment to their target arm to get it back to where it's supposed to be—all in the second and a half it takes to make a swing. As you can imagine the chances of success are not good.

As suggested above, one way to ensure that your target arm doesn't wander around while you swing is to plant it on your upper chest at address and leave it there. Imagine that there is a strip of Velcro on your chest and the strip on the underside of your target arm fits onto it, locking the two together. If you were to break the connection, you'd hear the famous Velcro *riiipppp*. Your job is to swing without any ripping.

But here is a danger you must avoid when trying to maintain connection. During your takeaway it's all too easy to let your arms turn the club inside your toe line—a position from which you probably can't recover. I want you to maintain connection but not at the expense of taking the club too much inside. Here is the guideline: At the end of your takeaway your club is parallel with the ground and directly over your toe line, with your target arm and wrist still in a straight line with the club shaft. Now you're well connected and ready to stay that way right to the finish.

■ *Stay in the Channel for a Perfect Takeaway*

To be sure you've made it through your takeaway correctly, lay two shafts parallel on the ground with the shaft closest to you on your

In the photo our model has started her swing with the club head low to the ground and her hands in the channel. With a little help from her instructor, she has accomplished this by moving her left shoulder down and out from her address position (note how her shoulders are now level) while she moves her hands and arms as a unit.

toe line. This forms a channel for your hands, and from the time you start your takeaway until it's completed, your hands should stay in the channel—neither moving inside or outside of it. A good way to check your position is to set up in front of a mirror and repeat your takeaway till it becomes automatic. Make sure to look in the mirror from the face on angle as well as from behind. Notice that a tee placed between your thumb and forefinger after you've taken your grip points to the sky as does the toe of the club face as you make your takeaway. This tells you that there has been no rolling or fanning of the hands to the inside.

From a proper setup position, with your hands in the channel created by the clubs on the ground, you're ready to start your takeaway, the movement of the club away from the ball. To do so let your arms swing across your chest until your target hand is just past your right foot. At this point with an iron your hands and the club head are the same height and are still in the channel. (With a driver the club head is a tad lower than the hands.) A common error during the takeaway is to roll your hands and forearms, causing your club face to open and the club head to get too deep behind you. From this position your only option is to lift the club to the top, destroying your coil and the path of your swing.

■ *The One-"Peace" Takeaway*

How do I get the club started?
This is a question I hear all the time from my students, and it's a good one. If you've watched tournaments on TV you've no doubt heard the analyst describe the "beautiful, one-piece takeaway" of a player, but you almost never hear exactly what makes it "one piece." Consequently when many golfers try to execute a one-piece takeaway, they concentrate on "one" element, like swinging the club handle or turning the left shoulder.

At address a line connecting my elbows and hands forms a triangle, and it should be maintained as the club swings away from the ball until my hands are past my right foot. After that (and it varies as to exactly when depending on your body build and grip pressure) the momentum of your arm swing will cock your wrists. This is the "one piece takeaway" you hear so much about. I like to call it the one-peace takeaway because it involves a simultaneous movement of the club head, hands, arms, shoulders, and chest as a unit. It looks un-manipulated and peaceful.

The fact is, however, that *one piece* doesn't refer to a single element of the swing. Zeroing in on a single body movement creates a jerky, inconsistent move away from the ball. To develop the correct concept, substitute the term *one peace* for *one piece*. Here's why this is helpful: In your golf swing, some movements are sequential and some are simultaneous. The one-piece takeaway is an example of a collection of simultaneous upper-body movements where the club head, hands, arms, and shoulders come away from the ball as a unit. Because there are no independent moving parts the motion is so coordinated that it looks peaceful. To do this you must make your chest the "master mover." All the other parts of your upper body can move independently of one another, but if you rotate your chest, everything moves. Think of your chest as the back of your triangle—to start your swing you simply rotate your chest so that your upper body swings away from the ball as a unit.

■ *Two Different Motions During the Backswing*

Too many golfers ruin their swing early in the backswing by keeping their arms glued to their sides as they whip their hands directly inside the toe line (an imaginary line connecting the toes that also represents the body line). Once your hands move inside your toe line during the takeaway, you'll have no choice but to "find" space for your hands and arms as they come back to the ball during the downswing by shoving the club away from your body. This misuse of space produces the cut-across action so common to slicers. To prevent an inside takeaway, create a window of space between your body and your trail arm.

It's a truism in the golf swing: That which goes in and then up must come out and then around—and that's exactly what happens when your hands swing quickly inside your toe line during the takeaway. As mentioned above, a good way to prevent this is to allow your trail elbow to float with the trail arm as the club head moves away from the ball, thereby opening a space between itself and your side. When your elbow remains fixed to your side, your club will pivot around it, taking the hands inside the toe line—a difficult position to recover from. The key to your takeaway, then, is to penetrate the depth dimension (the space behind your body line) only after you've completed your takeaway.

At waist high the left arm and wrist are still straight and the club is parallel with the ground—it has not been elevated by the wrist cock. Said another way, none of the height the club head has attained at this point is due to wrist cock. As I have said, from here, the club is set in position by your right arm folding.

One such angle is the relationship between your club's shaft and your left fore-arm (right forearm for left-handers). The formation of this angle is often termed "setting the angle" or, more simply, "cocking the wrists." Some good players set this angle early in their backswings; others set it very late. But regardless of when it is set, this angle is a prerequisite of a powerful swing. To get the feeling, simply hold the club in front of you (a), then pull back on the shaft as if you were cocking the hammer of a pistol (b).

■ Wrist Cock: The When, Why, and How

The golf swing is all about creating leverage to multiply your physical strength. By using leverage to your advantage, you may not be able to hit the ball three hundred yards, but you will be able to increase your club-head speed enough to send the ball a long way—but only if you take care to create certain angles of power in your swing.

An important power angle is created by moving your target wrist so your thumb travels toward your body, much as you would cock the hammer of a pistol. This simple movement creates leverage—a small input produces a large output. For an investment of about three inches of thumb movement, you'll get a return of three feet of club-head arc. Assuming you hold the angle correctly during the downswing, your investment will pay big dividends in the form of increased club-head speed just where you need it—at impact.

■ *When Does the Cock Occur?*

At what point in the backswing should you add that power-producing wrist cock to your swing? It depends. Some golfers, like Juli Inkster and Jack Nicklaus, cock their wrists late in their backswing and some, like Ernie Els and Jeff Maggert, cock them earlier. Be it late or early, the wrists must cock to create an angle between your left forearm (for right-handed players) and the club shaft. This angle gives you the power of leverage, an essential ingredient in adding force to motion. Levers are multipliers of power, and the human body is equipped with powerful levers that can be an integral part of your golf swing, if you know how to use them efficiently.

Think of it this way: During the initial stage of the backswing, the shaft is an extension of the target arm, straight with no bend. However, it's crucial that you set the angle between the shaft and your forearm by the time your arm is across the center of your chest. If the set is delayed any longer the club will simply be lifted to the top of your swing with the loss of coil. By cocking your wrists you elevate the club to the top of your backswing with minimal exertion as you maintain the powerful connection of your arms to your body. The leverage, or the angle that wrist cocking produces, literally multiples your strength when it is unleashed through impact in the form of club-head speed. You'll notice a huge increase in the distance your shots fly when you add this lever to your swing.

Generally, the momentum of a swing will cause the wrists to cock without your consciously attempting to make it happen, but if this doesn't happen naturally in your swing, use the following as a guideline for the when and how of wrist cock. Assuming normal flexibility and an average body build, when your hands reach waist high the left arm and wrist should retain the straight-line relationship that they had at address. At this point, since the wrists have yet to elevate the club head, the club shaft, at this point, is parallel to the ground. From here, you cock your wrists, creating an angle (usually 90 degrees) between your left arm and the club shaft. All the while, the front arm stays glued to your chest as the club travels to the top of your swing via your right elbow bending (another source of leverage).

Remember that this wrist cock and the folding of the right arm should happen in response to the momentum of the club head as it swings away from you. If it doesn't, you have to make it happen in your practice sessions until you train yourself to let it happen. Then you're ready to take it to the golf course.

■ It's Nine O'Clock, Do You Know Where Your Hands Are?

If you're like a lot of my students, when you're playing well, you think you'll never play badly again, and when you're playing badly, you're certain you'll never play well again. Neither belief is true, of course, but it brings up an interesting question: Why does your golf swing come and go on such a seemingly random basis? It appears to make no sense at all. Actually, part of the answer relates to *no sense*—the failure of your brain to sense where your hands are after they leave your visual field.

While you may not be consciously aware of it, your brain has no problem keeping track of your hands when they are in front of you because they are visible. You look directly at them at address and see them with your peripheral vision during the takeaway. And it is your hands, as the tactile center of your swing, that allow you to track the club head—-so you could say that your hands *are* the club head. But during your backswing, as your hands approach nine o'clock, they exit your visual field. To "see" the hands now, the brain must rely solely on its network of sensors throughout the body whose job it is to report what body parts are where.

Golf's "big three" are the ball, the target, and the club head, and since you don't look at either the target or the club head for the majority of every swing, you've lost visual contact with two of the big three. The problem is that when you suddenly deprive your brain of its dominant tracking system (sight), as you do at some point in every swing, it requires a smooth transition from your visual to your kinesthetic system to keep the club head going where it should. *And turning over every swing to your sense of feel is just asking for trouble. Unless you practice or play every day and are stress free, "feel" is a shaky edifice on which to build your swing.*

Here are two steps you can take to keep your good swing around as long as possible. First, make a blueprint of your good swing—-write down in detail what you do when you are swinging well. It may sound simple, but even Jack Nicklaus at the peak of his career had trouble doing it. He admits that when he discovers a swing key that works he often can't remember to use it the next day. He once told his caddie, "You've got to start writing these things down." And so do you. If you don't know what you're doing, see your PGA teaching pro and write down what she or he tells you. With your blueprint in hand, you can quickly reconstruct your swing when it starts to go south. Video is also a great help, but make sure you're swinging well for the camera. In addition to filming your full swing, zoom in on the various parts of your swing, like the takeaway or the top of your swing. Once you have your swing movie, salt it away until you need it. At the first sign of problems, tape your swing again and compare it to your model.

The second thing you can do to protect your swing is the following drill: Close your eyes and, from your normal address position, swing your hands to pocket height. Now open your eyes and check how near you came to perfection; then adjust and close your eyes to fix the feel. Repeat this closed-open-adjust-closed sequence with your hands at nine o'clock, both for the backswing and the downswing. This will help you make the transition from sight to feel without a hitch.

In photo (a) I'm in good position; in photo (b), my head is hanging over my left side. Letting your head float is a subtle move, but it's a part of every good swing. Older players, and/or those with less flexibility, let their head float even more. Just make sure that you don't overdo the head float; you need to *let* it happen, not *make* it happen.

■ At the Top of Your Swing

Let Your Head Float With Your Chest Turn

Too many golfers fail to make a good chest turn during their backswing, not because they don't want to but because they can't. It's a combination of anatomy and bad advice. Your head is fastened to your body, the final stop in the journey up the spinal cord. It can cock a bit from side to side, as when you're not exactly sure of something; nod up and down (the affirmative action), and rotate to either side, until the chin is over the shoulder line. It can also combine some of these movements à la Jack Nicklaus, who has always cocked and rotated his head to start his backswing, putting him immediately behind the ball, a position to be held until after the ball is gone.

Now that was his strategy for moving his head behind the ball, and it is unfortunate that he publicly advocated keeping the head fixed, because if you force yourself to keep your head stock-still bad things happen. If your head is normal, whether empty or full, it weighs about ten pounds. Basically that means that you've got ten pounds of downward pull suddenly created when your body turns out from under it; and it's this imbalance that causes your spine to bow toward the ball, creating a body tilt rather than a turn. By the way, the muscles of your neck are severely taxed holding your dangling head immobile at such an odd angle, and it's no wonder that a swing like this makes golf a pain in the neck.

A companion effect of the tilt is the feeble lifting of the arms in lieu of a fully coiled chest turn, and now we know the cause of these problems. It comes from that old dagger that drains the lifeblood out of even the most robust of golf swings—*Don't move your head*—so let's put it aside and replace it with a new prescription for head management: *Let your head float.*

In the photo on the right (b), I've turned my left shoulder, but my right has stayed in place. This is a "single shoulder turn" that causes me to simply lift the club with little coil. In the companion photo (a) I've turned both shoulders as I should—the left under my chin and the right behind my neck. This double turn multiplies the power dramatically.

■ Do You Have a Double Shoulder Turn?

No doubt influenced by the shearing that Butch Harmon gave Tiger Woods's swing, too many golfers are shortening their swings in the wrong way, that is, at the expense of shoulder turn. When they do it this way they shorten their swings, but they also lose a lot of distance and usually some accuracy. If you're specifically trying to shorten your swing or if you're having trouble making a correct shoulder turn, listen up.

Remember that your muscles don't like to stretch, and they'll find a way *not* to if you let them. It may be wrong, but it's much easier to skip the shoulder turn and simply lift the club up to the top of your swing by straightening your spine and bending your target arm. To be sure *both* shoulders turn properly you'll need to keep them moving at a 90-degree angle to your spine. When you do, your target shoulder moves down under your chin while your rear shoulder moves up behind the neck. Actually, your shoulders are making a level turn around your spine, but because your spine is inclined toward the ball, they are angled toward the ground.

To turn your shoulders correctly, first stand upright so your shoulders form a perpendicular line with your spine and are level to the ground. Rotate your chest back and forth, keeping your shoulders level to the ground. Next, if you bend from the waist into your golf posture and turn your chest in exactly the same way, you'll duplicate the motion required for your golf swing. The idea is to keep your shoulders perpendicular to your spine as they turn both back and through the ball.

The key here is that you don't make any effort to move your front shoulder down to the ball; tilt your left shoulder down and your weight stays on your front leg and never gets behind the ball, producing a swing error known as a *shoulder tilt*. Another temptation is to level your shoulders to the ground as you turn in your backswing. This straightens your spine and destroys your posture and relationship to the ball.

Here's a good checkpoint for your shoulder turn: Both at the top of your swing and just after impact, a line connecting your shoulders would be slanted at the same angle as your club shaft is at address.

■ *Flex Time*

Here is a very common mistake: At the top of the swing the golfer straightens his back leg, causing the hips to tilt and the front knee to jut out toward the target line. This creates a tilted body that must reposition itself perfectly during the downswing to repair the imbalances at the top—a difficult task in the less than half a second you have to reach impact. The solution is to flex that back leg at address and keep it that way as you swing to the top, then back to the ball.

Let's take an example we used earlier to show how destructive losing your body level can be. Say your five-iron is 38 inches long and your left arm is 32 inches from the tip of your shoulder to your knuckles, making a total length at address, shoulder to club head, of 70 inches. Ignoring for the moment the effects of physics such as the bowing of the shaft, your assignment is to produce solid contact by returning to impact with the same-length club as you started with—70 inches. If you overflex your legs, you'll come to impact with 71 inches and bury your club head in the ground behind the ball in a bone-jarring collision that leaves your ball well short of the target. If you *lose* the flex in your legs, the length is shortened to 69 inches, and you'll catch the very top of the ball, sending it skimming along the ground. If you want to play your best, most consistent golf, keep the flex in your knees you created at address all the way to impact.

■ *The Overall Position at the Top*

As shown in the swing sequence on page 54, the backswing is made up of two parts: the *takeaway,* where the club head starts away from the ball, creating width and leverage; and the *upswing,* where the club head continues its journey by rising to the top of the swing. The combination of the two (away and up) produces the height and swing arc you need for power.

■ The Upswing

As I discussed in the beginning of this chapter, the takeaway sets the stage for the upswing. Once it's complete, all that remains to be done is to turn your chest away from the target, allowing your front shoulder to move under your chin and your back shoulder to move behind your neck. This along with the folding of your back elbow brings the club to the top of the swing. At the top of our model's backswing, his shoulders are fully turned and his elbows are level with one another. The club is supported by both hands with the club face in a square position—pointing at the same angle as his target arm. The angle of his trail arm matches his spine angle showing that he has not raised up at the top of his swing. Both feet are flat on the ground, providing traction so his upper body can coil against a resisting lower body. The amount of hip and shoulder rotation he achieves at this point is a function not only of technique but also of his level of flexibility.

Note the beautiful turn and also the flare of both feet. When the front foot is flared out at address, it's easier to rotate your front hip and knee correctly through the hitting zone. A flared back foot will allow you to turn behind the ball, giving you increased rotation on the backswing.

■ The Forward Swing to Impact

The move that starts the downswing is really two moves, one lower body and one upper body. Starting down, your target arm slides toward your back foot. There's only so much *down* and so much *around* in every swing. The correct sequence is first to let the club move down, and then it moves forward to the ball. The key to striking the ball solidly is keeping this sequence. Unfortunately, it's common for golfers in their anxiety to reverse the sequence. They turn their chest (the *around* part) before they move the club down, so the club moves out toward the target line while it is still very high. Then, as it drops to the ball, it's on the cut-across path to the ball. It's an error called *over the top,* and when you make this mistake there will be a slice in your portfolio of shots.

If you move the club down first, about halfway to the ball your target arm is parallel to the ground with your back still to the target. Here's where your back knee begins its kick toward the target as your back elbow and hip grow closer to one another. Thus the trailing side resists while the leading side pulls, maintaining the coil and even increasing it as you start down.

In the photo the full extension of both my arms shows that the club head was fully released to the ball so that just after impact, my left arm is straight and in front of my body. Notice how my left arm is still connected to my chest with no breakdown at the elbow, an indication that my club head stayed on the correct path.

Through the impact zone, our model is nicely behind the golf ball. His back heel hasn't flipped up, showing that he has allowed his right side to release but hasn't twisted his back shoulder up and over the ball. He's on his front heel and the outer rim of his foot, indicating a correct weight transfer. At this point he has about 80 percent of his weight on his front side ready to act as a buttress or wall of resistance against which he will hit.

Just before impact, his lead hip has rotated behind him, increasing the force on the club head. His lead arm is straight while his trailing arm is still slightly bent in order to retain the wrist cock until the very last moment. At impact his trail arm fully straightens in a powerful release, dumping all the force into the ball.

There are two important points to make note of concerning your approach to the ball. The first is that while your lead arm slides down your chest and your trailing arm straightens, you maintain the 90-degree angle between your lead forearm and the club shaft. This is an angle of power that must be held until the impact zone. The second is that you must start your downswing by transferring pressure into your front hip; otherwise you're stranded in your back hip and your swing becomes too steep. If your swing is correctly rounded, just after impact both your arms will be fully extended—the only time in the golf swing when both are straight.

Starting Down—in Detail

The transfer of weight I highlighted above is a subtle movement similar to shifting your weight while dancing; it is a distribution based on the rhythm of the moment, and while you can't focus on it while you play, you can prepare for it while you practice using the drill outlined herein.

At every golf seminar or golf school I teach, I get the same question: "How do I start the downswing?" Before I answer it in specifics I always outline the goal as follows: Your goal, if you want a consistently correct swing, is to be "in" the correct hip socket at the correct time as your swing unfolds. I use the word *in* to mean that you have established that hip joint as the center of rotation by shifting weight into it and then turning your body around it. Or, said another way, to give yourself the best chance to hit a good golf shot, you need to be *in* your back hip joint during your backswing and *in* your forward hip joint during your forward swing.

To start your downswing, your weight is flowing into your front hip, but there is more to the story than that. Think of it this way: Obviously at the top of your swing your hands are "up there," and the ball is "down there," so whatever else you do, your hands–clubhead package must come down—*that's why they call it the downswing.*

As we discussed above, there are two moves, inseparable companions from the start, that occur when your lead arm falls back down your chest as your weight shifts from your back leg to your front one. Just as your lead arm swung across and up your chest to begin your backswing, it now reverses its path to start your downswing.

■ The Drill

Here is a drill that will give you the feel of this dynamic arm drop–weight-shift duet. First of all, tee up all shots. Using a seven-iron address your ball as you normally do, making sure to play the ball in the middle of your stance. Then draw your front foot to your back one until the heels almost touch, leaving your club face soled behind the ball. To begin the drill, swing your club back until your target arm is parallel with the ground, at which point you start your downswing by stepping back into your setup position. As soon as your front foot hits the ground, your arms–club-head package drops to hit the ball.

■ One Thing to Watch For

As soon as your weight is deposited in your front hip, your hips take over your swing and begin a powerful rotation, your front hip serving as the center for the rotation. Doing this drill you should be careful because it's all too easy to simply slide your hips toward the target and never turn them in time. From the top, your hips move laterally toward the target until the weight is deposited in the front hip joint. At this point, the front hip begins its rotation.

■ *The Hip Switch*

There aren't a lot of fundamentals in this game. Most of the so-called fundamentals are negotiable—there are many ways to hold a club, many stances that work, and so on. But one of the few nonnegotiables is that there's a weight switch in every good golf swing. That is, at the top of the swing, a high proportion of the weight is in the back hip, while at the beginning of the downswing the switch is made to the front hip.

Golf is a rotational game because you must, by rule, stand to the side of the ball. It's fundamental that you have pivot points to rotate around. Here's a rule of thumb about your pivot points: When you're swinging away from the ball, you should be shifting weight onto your trail leg; when you're swinging to the ball, your weight should be shifting onto your front leg. Exactly how much weight should you transfer back and forth? It depends on your size, strength, and flexibility, as well as the club you're using, but let's use the figure 80 percent with the driver, less with irons and very little with the sand wedge.

To get the feeling, place a board that's strong enough to support your weight over an old golf shaft or broomstick, forming a teeter totter. Stand on the board and take your stance with a teed five-iron so that the board touches the ground on the left side. Make a few slow-motion swings and feel the board incline at the top of your swing where it touches the ground on the right side. Take care to turn rather than slide your hips. Now as you start back to the ball the board tilts to the left side, setting up your left hip as the pivot center for the downswing. This teaches you a fundamental: Weight in a hip joint creates a rotational center.

■ *The Advantage of the Hip Switch—Slotting the Club*

You may not have thought about it, but gravity has a significant effect on your golf swing. The "effort" part of your swing should be the backswing, because in it you must overcome the force of gravity as you take the club back to the top. That's the bad news. The good news is that once your club reaches the top of your backswing, it's poised to take advantage of the very force that was working against it a moment before—all you have to do is let it happen.

Unfortunately, most weekend golfers aren't willing to let gravity take over and instead force the club back toward the ball with the upper right quadrant of the body. This burst of energy occurs at precisely the wrong point in the swing, pushing the club head out toward the target line and resulting in a swing destined to produce a pull or pull slice.

What is called for at the top of your swing is a downward drop of the arms and club, a movement that precedes any upper-body turning. All you have to do is switch hips and then do nothing. Think of it as a surrender to gravity that drops your club into proper position before it begins its journey forward toward the ball. Once your club has dropped, you can then make a strong turn back to the target, assured that your club is on a powerful path to the ball.

To get the feeling of letting your club fall down the "gravity gradient," hit a few practice balls while trying to drop your hands onto your right foot before you allow your upper body to move. It should feel as if your hands are moving in slow motion at the start of the downswing. Be sure to maintain your wrist cock and to let your trail arm straighten as your hands drop toward the ground.

Although you might feel as though you will release the club too late at impact, this is exactly how a correct swing feels when you surrender to gravity. After all, that's why it's called the "downswing" and not the "around swing."

■ What's Going On With Your Chest

Just after David Duval and Annika Sorenstam are in the thick of things during a televised Tour event, the lesson books of golf instructors all over the country fill up, because golfers try to copy these great players. Their chests seem to turn to the target to start the downswing; to the naked eye it looks like their chests snap around to bring the club to the ball. Despite appearances, don't be fooled—if you actually used your chest like this you'd hit about the biggest push slice you can imagine and then (as you should) you'd go to see your PGA teaching professional.

The eye is fooled in this case because good players don't spin their chests to hit the ball; in fact, as stop-action photos demonstrate, the arms and club head must get back in front of the midline of the body at impact to constantly produce a square club face. But when you start your chest turning too early, your arms can never catch up, and you'll either have to flip your hands to square the club face or it will be wide open on contact and the ball will slice. Jack Nicklaus's swing key for this all-important position was "buttons to ball," meaning that at impact he had the feeling that the buttons of his shirt were pointing at the ball. If you did this there is no way your chest could beat your club head to the ball.

■ Forget the Late Hit—What You Want Is the Late Entry

In their haste to hit the ball, most golfers apply pressure on the shaft prematurely just as they start their downswing. They are anxious to get the club head on the target line very early in the downswing. That's understandable, because that's where the ball is. In this case the closer the club head gets to impact, the more the turn works against the player, because it pulls the club across the target line in a side-swiping arc. This is exactly the situation you *don't* want—the better your turn, the worse the shot. Remember that to hit a good shot from a bad position, you have no choice but to make a bad swing. And you can't play your best golf from bad positions because the law of averages will catch up with you.

You want to be in a position during your downswing where you turn works for you—this way, the better your turn, the better the shot. To make your turn work for you, you need the correct downswing path: Your club head comes from inside the target line, and, as it approaches the ball, turns onto the target line so that it looks directly at the target in time for impact.

To help you do the above, lay down two clubs one on either side of the ball to form a channel. *Your goal during your downswing is to keep your club head out of the channel as long as you can. Forget the late hit, you want a late entry.* You want to keep the club head off the target line until the last instant—the longer the better. It will feel like the ball is going to right field, but be patient, because if you're aimed properly, you'll get the hang of it after about twenty balls.

■ Special Delivery

There are many ways to swing a golf club, but great players have one thing in common—they deliver the club to the ball on the correct path. In a good golf swing, the club shaft approaches the ball from between the toe line and the target line. Mistakes are made when the shaft approaches too severely from inside the target line, or too much from the outside. Good players tend to err on the inside track— the club gets too shallow, and the butt end of the shaft points right of target as they approach the ball. High handicappers tend to approach from the outside and the butt points left of target during an approach that is too steep.

Tour players Mike Hill (a) and Kermit Zarley (b) demonstrate how to get the club in the "pro slot." The success of your shot in large part is the result of proper aim and alignment, proper coil, and the patience to let your swing unwind at its own pace. Unfortunately, in a misguided effort to generate power, many high handi-cappers begin the downswing with a violent move of the back shoulder, which forces the club outside the target line and produces slices and pulls. Our models illustrate the correct way to begin the downswing. After creating terrific coil at the top they simply allow the club to drop straight down until the left arm is parallel to the ground. This way the club approaches the ball from inside the target line and you cause the powerful muscles of the torso to deliver the club head into the back of the ball.

For each flaw, there is a compensating motion that develops over time—"insiders" learn to flip their hands through impact to keep the ball from going right, while "outsiders" learn to hold on and "chicken wing" to keep the ball from going left. Neither move is good, because it requires the conscious manipulation of the club, and cannot be done efficiently during an entire round of golf.

The best drill to cure path problems is the "drop" drill. From the top of the backswing start your downswing with two simultaneous motions—your weight transfers into your target hip while your hands drop straight down to hip height. At this point, your entire club shaft should be framed between the target line and the toe line. A tip for slicers: Don't let your right shoulder move until the club has made its drop. A tip for hookers: Make sure you allow your hips to turn prior to releasing the club.

■ Train Your Target Arm to Banish the Slice

Failure to rotate your forearms correctly through impact leaves the face open through the hitting area with the left palm facing the ground. The outcome is a slice.

The second cause of a slice results from sliding the upper body forward on the downswing, prompting the front elbow to jut out (chicken-wing), a move that also opens the face of your club. Cure these two slice moves and you've got a good chance to hit the ball straight.

To train your front arm to work properly, do front-arm-only swings while holding your upper arm against your side with your trail arm. Make sure that you keep your upper body back while you do this drill and feel how pinning your upper front arm causes it to fold naturally as you follow through. This rotates your front forearm and puts you in the palm-up position. If your front arm is trained properly your trail arm will extend after impact and rotate over your left.

Most golfers leave the club face open at impact because they fail to release their front forearm properly. To see the evidence of a good release take a look at my swing in the photos. At this point (about halfway between impact and finish) my trail arm is fully extended with my forearms, and my front forearm and wrist have rotated so that the palm of my hand is facing upward (this is called supination).

For the draw, your right forearm and hand are on top of your left with your right-hand knuckles to the sky, indicating a full release of the hands and arms through the hitting zone with the toe of the club rotating over the heel. The club is tilted away from the target line with the club head pointing well left of the target. To fade the ball, simply reverse everything.

■ Impact

There are no golf gods, just physics, geometry, and the human mind—a powerful if somewhat unstable combination when it comes to playing golf. The story is told of a famous teacher called to Saudi Arabia to teach the king of that country the game of golf. Not long into the lessons the king, exasperated at his poor shots in front of his ever-present retinue, threw a temper tantrum. "Your

Highness," said the teacher, summing up the allure of the game, "you know you're the king, and we know you're the king, but the ball doesn't know you're the king." And it doesn't care. All it cares about is what your club is doing at impact; its face position, angle of attack, club path, the squareness of contact, and the speed of the club head determine the spin and speed of your golf ball and ultimately its distance and direction. The bottom line is that your ball only knows impact.

■ Impact Is a Zone

So here is a drill that will help you get the feel of what should happen at the bottom of your swing, not at the high speeds of a real swing but at a very low speed. I define impact as a zone rather than a point, and that zone is approximately the width of your feet with club-ball contact coming somewhere in between.

Use a seven-iron and tee the ball where you normally would for a full swing. Position another tee on the target line opposite your back foot. Now extend the index finger of your lowest hand down the shaft and swing the club back and through, tracing the tee line with your index finger. Once you can do this, put a ball on the tee and actually hit the ball, taking care to keep your swing no longer than the distance between your feet.

Next make a full swing over the tee allowing your forearm to rotate through impact as shown above. If you don't hit the ball solidly, go back to step one and refocus on the square club face at impact, then move to the next step again. Do this until you can consistently hit a soft draw with your full swing.

■ The Wall at Impact

At the start of the downswing, the majority of your weight should be in your back hip joint with your front leg still flexed. As you near impact your front leg straightens to form a wall that you hit over. As the leg elongates, it serves as a brace to foster the rotation of the hips and shoulders, allowing the club head to speed to the ball as the 90-degree angle between the front arm and club shaft is lost. You want to feel as if your front knee is moving directly *away* from the target line during impact, rather than sliding *toward* the target. Golfers who are not hitting the ball as far as they ought to should monitor the action of their front leg. If it's late or fails to straighten at all, power leaks out of your swing just before impact.

Look at any long hitter (Davis Love, Annika Sorenstam, Phil Mickelson, and Tiger Woods are good examples) and you'll see that he or she has an almost straight front leg through impact. In other words, the front wall formed by the leg and hip is in place setting up a powerful collision between the club head and the ball. If you're losing your front-side brace, practice straightening your front leg through impact, just like a javelin thrower does when launching the javelin.

But before you practice your downswing position, make sure that you're loaded up behind the ball the way you should be at the top of your swing. At the top keep the flex you had in your front knee at address and let the knee be pulled away from the target so a line from your knee to the target line would be slightly behind the ball. It is only after the front arm slides back down your chest that your front leg begins to firm up until, just before impact, the club head is a blur, indicating that it's moving much faster than the rest of the body.

■ *A Problem Just Before Impact: Coming Over the Bottom*

Here is a problem that's hard to spot if you're not looking for it. Let me set the stage with a little background. Your shoulders should not be level at address. The rule of thumb is that your front shoulder should be higher than your back shoulder by the same amount that your top hand is higher than your bottom hand. During your swing the shoulders turn around your spine at an angle because your spine is tilted. Thus on the backswing your target shoulder gets lower and your trail shoulder higher. Now on the downswing it is just the reverse: As you come down your shoulders retrace their steps on essentially the same arc they took on the backswing. Any change in the spine incline just before impact changes the arc the shoulders travel on, thereby dislodging the club head from its path and ruining impact.

This leveling of the shoulders just before impact I call "coming over the bottom," and while it is difficult to see with the naked eye, it causes the same problems in ball flight (pulls and pull slices) as its cousin, the familiar and more easily spotted error called "coming over the top," which occurs at the start of the downswing. The solution to coming over the bottom is simple—keep your spine angle through the impact zone.

▨ A Common Problem at Impact: Your Chicken Wing

Trying simply to fix the chicken wing won't work. It's usually a result of a bad path, which itself can have a number of causes, one of which mentioned above is called "coming over the top," a move that occurs in the transition from backswing to downswing. It's pretty normal to want to kill the ball, but the problem is you don't want to do it from the start of your downswing. When you do, your hands and your trail shoulder, instead of moving downward, start out toward the ball, pushing your club head well outside the path you established in your backswing.

Now with this cut-across path you've got two choices. The first is to release the club head aggressively, squaring the club head to the ball, but the problem is that with the club traveling from outside to in, releasing the club face produces a wild shot that flies far left of target. And believe me, it won't take too many of those off-the-edge-of-the-world pulls before you start unconsciously chicken-winging, where you hold the face open by bending your target arm so that it's forced away from its powerful connection to your chest. This leaves you with a side-swiping action that cuts severely across the ball, causing a weak slice.

■ De-Wing Your Swing

To keep your club on the path and stop the chicken wing, make sure to be patient as your downswing unfolds. If you're in a reasonable position at the top of your swing, you must exercise some self-control—there is no impact before it's time. Allow yourself only one fast point in your swing and save it for the ball. Any pressure placed on the shaft as you start down shoves it out toward and then across the target line. This creates the two options outlined above, both of which are unacceptable if good golf is what you're about.

When you have a problem you need to fix the cause first (in this case a bad path) before you can focus on the result (the chicken wing). So the first step in ridding yourself of the chicken wing is to keep your trail shoulder and hands from moving outward to start the downswing. Actually, the hands and arms move down and away from the trail shoulder, allowing the club time to get back in front of you at impact.

Once your path is fixed all you have to do is train yourself not to chicken-wing your target arm. To do this I suggest you pose in the position demonstrated in photo (b) on page 7, and then start your swing from it with the goal of returning to this fully extended position past impact. Hit enough balls using this drill until your swing is de-winged.

Our two models (pro golfers Jack Nicklaus and Pam Kerrigan) demonstrate the correct finish of a golf swing. (1) Your weight should be balanced in your front hip, so you can lift your back toe off the ground without redistributing your weight. (2) Your chest and back knee should be pointing at the target. (3) Your hands should be up above your front shoulder.

The Finish

■ *Pose and Repose*

How you finish your swing has a lot to say about whether the swing was good or bad. If you finish in the right position, it often means you made the right moves in order to arrive there. What are the three keys to a proper finish? One, your weight should be balanced in your front hip, so you can lift your back toe off the ground without redistributing your weight. Two, your chest and back knee should be pointing at the target. Three, your hands should be up above your front shoulder.

There are two common faulty finishes. The first occurs when your hands end up even with or below your front shoulder, with your weight teetering out of control on your front heel. This indicates that your swing was too flat. To fix the problem, place your body in the position of a good finish—hands high, body balanced and facing the target. From that position, swing the club backward to the top of your backswing in slow motion. It should feel as though the path the club head is moving on is much more upright, closer to a Ferris wheel than a merry-go-round. Then swing the club back down and through to your good finish, all in slow motion. Repeat this until you've got the feeling grooved.

The second faulty finish is the opposite of the first: You end up off balance with your weight moving away from the target, stranded on your back foot because your swing was too upright. Again start by posing in a good finish position, then swing backward slowly on a flatter path (more merry-go-round than Ferris wheel) until you reach the top. Repeat this until you're familiar with the feeling.

If you regularly finish poorly, you can benefit from this pose-and-repose drill, which, when done sixty times a day for twenty-one days in a row, will go a long way toward alleviating the problem.

■ *Your Driver and Your Fairway Woods*

The biggest mistake you can make with the driver is not having a feel for what you want to do when you swing. Don't rush two or three practice swings that are nothing like the way you want to swing the club. The practice swing isn't just a warm-up, it's part of your overall swing. Making good practice swings is an art. Watch

Davis Love: He takes his practice swing as if he were hitting the ball, and so should you.

A big part of hitting your driver well is related to what you do before you set the club in motion, so before we cover the driver swing I'll outline some preswing mechanics for your driver.

■ Stance Width

Most books advise keeping your feet shoulder-width apart, but I recommend a slightly wider stance, about one inch outside the shoulders as measured from the heels. I think this wide stance will help you improve your balance.

■ Alignment

The shoulder closest to the target should point parallel to the target line and left of the target while your feet should be square to the target line. This way it's easier to get your left side turning correctly during the downswing.

■ Weight Distribution

Since you want your weight behind the ball at the top of your backswing, you should put most of it there at address—about 70 percent. Then all you have to do is turn with a small weight shift and you're fully loaded for the downswing.

■ A Driver Swing Thought

Your only thought with the driver should be about shoulder turn. On the backswing, think about turning your front shoulder to your

---

WINDY TIP

To hit an extra-long driver downwind, move the ball up off your left toe and tee it up a little higher to make sure you catch it on the upswing.

---

chin, and then on the downswing turning your back shoulder to your chin. Note: Too many golfers let the chin go to the shoulder; instead, always let the shoulder go to the chin.

■ The Fairway Woods

Most golfers need more distance not only off the tee but from the fairway as well. Granted, there is no one solution to the distance problem—it involves having properly fitting equipment, playing from the correct tees, a sound swing combined with a certain amount of strength, and flexibility that comes through special training. I'll focus on an area of the game especially vital to those who don't hit the ball a long way off the tee—the fairway woods.

The biggest mistake I see amateurs make with the fairway woods is trying to hit up on the ball. They're worried about getting the ball airborne, so they try to help it get there by lifting up with their bodies. Unfortunately, the result is just the opposite, a topped shot, followed by more lifting, followed by another topped shot. You can break out of this cycle of error by trusting the loft of your fairway wood to do its job. Remember the key: Hit down with a sweeping motion on your fairway woods.

The correct address is very important to good fairway-wood play, so here are some basics:

Ball position. To help you hit down on the ball, address the ball about two inches back from your left heel opposite the logo of your shirt.

Stance width. Your stance should be square with your feet, about shoulder-width apart (measured from the heels).

Alignment. Be careful to set your shoulders so they point slightly left of your target. This way, they will have to travel farther to reach full coil on the backswing, and you'll be sure to start your downswing with your lower body because your shoulders will still be turning back.

Weight distribution. About 25 percent of your weight should be on your left side, 75 percent on your right. Even though you should concentrate on hitting down on the ball, you still need a sufficient weight shift to hit the ball a long way.

■ *An Important Swing Thought*

I think that one reason the fairway woods are so hard for the average player to hit is that the distance is such a long shot, players often have no specific target in mind. When you're lining up your shot, pick an area where you want your ball to land and then visualize the flight of the ball. Always have a clear picture in your mind of exactly what it is you want the ball to do.

Though you don't make a conscious effort to change your swing, the flatter swing plane of a fairway wood produces a sweeping motion through the ball, a motion that requires a decent lie to pull off the shot. The more the ball sits on top of the grass, the more you can sweep it without taking a divot. But too many golfers try to hit their three-wood out of poor lies, and that's asking for trouble. So make it a rule to use your three-wood from a good lie, but when the ball sits down in the grass, especially in the rough, opt for your five- or seven-wood. Because their shafts are slightly shorter and your ball position isn't as forward, you'll contact the ball with the descending motion necessary to get your ball airborne.

Your lofted fairway woods also feature small heads specially designed to keep the club moving smoothly through the ball even in the rough. Remember, though, you don't change your swing motion. Just let the club's design get the ball in the air.

■ *U Makes You Better*

The fairway woods are designed to sweep the ball off the grass. There is no divot because the ball is hit at the bottom of the swing arc. The club head should be swinging level to the ground at the moment of impact. This is called a "shallow angle of attack," where the club head makes a gradual approach to the ball—more like an airplane landing than a parachute dropping straight down. You can promote a shallow angle of attack by adjusting your setup. It's not the same one you use for iron shots, which are designed to take a divot.

A Make sure you have the entire sole plate (the bottom surface) of your club head on the ground. This establishes the correct shaft angle for address, and you can build the rest of your stance around it.

B Set your right shoulder lower than your left.

C Check your head position. If you've done all the above it will be behind the ball.

If the butt of the club points directly at the ground during your downswing, your swing is too abrupt—more like a V than a U. The only way to level off (the flat portion of the U) just before impact is to point the butt of the club at the ball.

To be a good fairway-wood player, make sure to transfer your weight to your rear foot during the backswing. To start your downswing, shift your weight to your front foot, allowing your back shoulder to move down (not out toward the target) as your arms fall. This sequence is critical because to have a shallow angle of attack into the ball, you must have the "down" portion of your swing started before the "forward" portion takes place. Think of your swing as being U-shaped; you want to swing down the side of the U first before the club head moves along the flat part of the U to the ball.

Once you've done the down part allow your spine to rebound a bit away from the target as you approach the ball—this tilt is a natural result of the club swinging past you. When you keep your tilt you can extend through impact and turn up the other side of the U so you finish in full balance.

CHAPTER 4

Chipping and Pitching

The Difference Between a Chip and a Pitch

Many golfers don't know when to pitch and when to chip. They're two different shots with different techniques, and knowing when to use them can lower your scores. A sure sign that you're confusing the two types of shots is when your green-side shots are routinely getting caught in the fringe or running too far past the hole.

Think of your pitch shot as your air route to the flag, while your chip travels mostly on the ground. Since it's easier to judge a rolling ball versus a high flyer, if you're within six paces of the green, chip the ball; if you're more than six paces from the green and there's trouble (like rough) between you and the green, you should pitch the ball. Once you know how to chip and pitch, you'll be able to tell which technique to use quite easily, but please remember that six yards is a general guideline—you might chip from thirty yards (down a mound with nothing between you and the hole) and sometimes you'll pitch from three yards (when your ball is buried deep in Bermuda grass).

The Pitch

Choose your most lofted club, usually your sand wedge, for your pitch shots. No matter how long your pitch shot is, always line up the butt end of the club with the center of your body. Not only does this position maintain proper loft on the club face but it gives you a simple goal while you swing. Keep the butt of the club in the center of the body.

Your ball position moves back of center for low-flying pitches; middle for normal height; to forward, off your front heel, for the lob shot (the highest type of pitch shot, sometimes known as the "son-of-a-pitch" because it's so hard to hit correctly).

The triangle formed by your shoulders and arms remains intact until about waist height; you must relax your wrists so they'll be

When you pitch, your body turns and your wrists cock, just like in your full swing. The amount of weight shift and knee action depend on the length of the shot—it's something you learn by practice.

cocked by the weight of your swinging club head. Only when your trail elbow begins to fold do your wrists cock, and the more it folds, the higher the ball flies.

■ The Standard Pitch Shot

The pitch shot is a valuable scoring weapon that can turn three shots into two in a hurry. It's especially useful on par-5s, where you lay up short of the green with your second shot in position to hit a pitch of, say, 30 to 60 yards. Now the distances for the pitch will vary, depending on a player's strength, but usually the long pitch with the sand wedge travels about 20 yards shorter than a full sand wedge, whereas the short pitch may be only a few feet. So if your full-swing sand wedge flies 80 yards, your maximum long-pitch shot would be 60 yards. My advice is to get really good at pitching the ball, because that's where the birdies and pars are. Figure it this way: Say the par-5 is 490 yards, and without forcing anything you hit your drive 230 yards and your lay-up second shot travels 200 yards, leaving you 60 yards. Now let's suppose there are four par-5s. If you follow this strategy and put your ball in position, it's like playing four par-3s of 60 yards each.

■ The Pitch-Swing Motion

For any length pitch, you'll rotate both your chest and shoulders back and through. As the shot continues to increase in length the final power source, the hips, becomes the focal point of your swing, and you shift your weight from hip to hip as your hands swing to about shoulder height. For medium to short pitches, there is rotation but no weight shift.

Play the ball in the middle of your stance with your weight favoring your target leg—about 60 percent weight to the front leg, 40

Allow the center of the chest to rotate out from under your head as you keep your head still and back behind the ball. Too many golfers suddenly stop their arms and body just before impact in an attempt to put a "hit" on the ball. This collapses the target-side wrist, sending the club head shooting past the hands at just the wrong time. I keep everything moving through the ball at the same speed. In other words, I simply hit this type of shot with your turn, eliminating any ruinous bursts of power.

percent back leg. When you execute the pitch shot, you apply no conscious "hit" to the ball because your swing is smooth. The force is generated by the constant acceleration of the club head and the length of your swing.

The triangle formed by the shoulders and arms at address is re-formed through impact, ensuring that the ball starts on the correct line to the flag. Allow the chest to rotate as you swing back to the ball so the club head stays behind the hands until just before impact. This ensures that there will be no flippiness through impact, so the club face stays on line. Coming through without flipping the wrists allows you to slip the club face under the ball, unlocking every bit of loft that's in the sand wedge.

As you take your stance, aim your club face to the left of target, then open it a bit so it points at the target. Play from a wide-open stance where your body line (represented by your toe line) is at least 30 degrees open. As you start your backswing, cock your wrists (a) and make sure to swing your hands along your body line. This produces a cut-across swing that slides the sand wedge under the ball. Take care not to allow your trail forearm to cross over the front as you do in a normal full swing. When you finish your pitching swing, you should be able to look directly at the face of your club—if there were a mirror on your club face, you could see your reflection in it. Check out our junior model in photo (b); his club face is looking directly at him.

Low-Running Pitch

Most of the time we think of the pitch shot as a high-arching shot with not much roll to it—a shot that stops shortly after it lands. But for maximum control, when you have some green to work with, the best shot is the pitch and run, a low shot that spends most of its time on the ground. Most often this shot is used from close range, when you have to carry a bit of tough terrain, land on the green, and run to the hole. To put a number to it, you're five or so steps off the green, and while it can be used from much farther out with a slight modification of technique, I'll focus here on the short pitch and run.

If you swing in balance you'll find your hands never rise above waist height on the backswing for a short pitch. But remember to

The low pitch shot rolls a considerable distance after it hits the green. It's an ideal shot to play when the pin is on the second tier and you need to run your ball up the slope to the flag. It's also a great shot on a windy day, when you want to keep your shot as low as possible. Note the short-to-long action; this ensures that you make contact with the accelerating club head.

swing your arms with a bit of body turn instead of just lifting them into position. The key to the pitch and run is your back elbow—it remains relatively straight (but not stiff) with only a slight bend. This allows your hands, arms, and club head to stay low with almost no wrist cock, a very accurate way to pitch. Experiment with the club you choose—since it depends on the height and how much run you want, it could be anywhere from a nine-iron to a sand wedge.

I've outlined the technique for the standard pitch shot, where you choose your most lofted club (your sand wedge) for your pitch shots. I suggested that no matter how long your pitch shot is, always line up the butt end of the club with the center of your body. Not only does this position maintain proper loft on the club face but it gives you a simple goal while you swing—keep the butt in the center of the body.

But you must make several adjustments to hit the running pitch shot correctly. Instead of your sand wedge, use a pitching wedge or even a nine-iron, because the reduced loft will keep the ball down out of the wind. Move the ball about two inches back of the center of your stance and make sure to aim the club face at your target first. Then take your stance to ensure that your shoulders are slightly closed, the way they should be for a back ball position. The big mistake most golfers make when they move the ball back in their stance is to aim too far to the right without realizing it, so be on your guard.

As to the swing itself, the big difference is that you let your forearms release exactly as you do for a regular shot, which as we have seen is different for the normal pitch shot, where the club face never turns over.

Remember your pitch is moving slower than a full shot, so the wind will have much more of an effect. Most golfers realize that the low runner is a good shot to play into the wind, but it's usually only the expert who plays the running pitch shot *down*wind—a good choice because the wind behind your back often takes the spin off the ball, making it very hard to stop a high pitch close to the hole, no matter how much you clip it.

■ Weight Shift and Rotation

There's no time in a short swing for a weight transfer, so your foot width is narrower than your hip width, and your weight stays in your front hip joint, where it settles naturally when you drop your front foot back. But just because you're not shifting doesn't mean you should stand stone-still and just swing your arms up and down. Let your body rotate around your front hip axis as you swing the club.

■ The Swing

The Y formed by your arms and club shaft remains intact throughout your swing. In order to do this you must keep your chest moving from start to finish, with the butt of your club pointing at your chest even after the ball has landed. As with any pitch, you don't want the club head to pass your hands through impact. The most common mistake made in pitching is to abruptly stop the arms at impact in an attempt to put a "hit" on the ball. You can avoid this by keeping your arms and chest moving together into your follow-through. For the pitch and run, the length of your backswing is always shorter than the length of your follow-through.

■ The Lob

When hitting a high, soft lob, don't let the short distance trick you into a short backswing. The image word for the lob is *syrupy,* and your concept of the shot should be *full turn with minimum power.* The key to the lob is to make a silky, flowing swing, moving the club face with the rotation of your body, without any manipulation by your arms or hands.

The lob shot should be used only under special circumstances, but it's one of those shots that can energize your round by allowing you to save par or make birdie from dire circumstances. As I've said it's easier to judge a rolling ball than a high flying one, so here is my advice when choosing a shot: putt it first; if you can't putt it, chip it; if you can't chip it, pitch it; and only when you have to, lob it. The lob is the hardest of the short shots to judge, but it is often your only choice if you wish to carry over trouble (bunkers, water, etc.) and settle softly next to the pin.

The lob requires a full-body rotation, much the same as your regular swing, except that you cut way back on the speed of your turn, and you don't release your hands through impact. Since your body leads the way throughout your swing, your club head stays trapped behind you and, therefore, remains open through impact. This allows the bounce on the bottom of your sand wedge to slide gently under the ball as you swing to a full finish.

One common mistake is to swing the club using a long backswing, a short, decelerated downswing, and an abbreviated follow-through. This long-to-short action is a good way to leave the ball in the long grass, or dump it into the hazard you were trying to carry. A second common mistake is to make a short, quick swing by trying to match the length of the swing to the length of the shot as you would for pitches, chips, and putts. You can convince your brain that a long swing works with such a short shot by hitting a lot of 15- to 20-yard pitches on the driving range until you can produce the high, soft trajectory every time.

Everything about the lob setup is designed to produce a high, soft shot. Begin your setup by aiming the club face directly at the target, and then align your body square to the target line. Position the ball off the instep of your target foot, and make sure that the butt end of your golf club is in the midline of your body. Open your stance dramatically so your body faces left of the target, and with your heels about shoulder width, anchor the majority of weight in your front hip joint. This establishes your front hip as the rotational center throughout your swing. The most common error is setting the hands ahead of the club face, which reduces the loft on the club face—just what you don't want.

Once your setup is complete, the operational word that governs your swing is *rotation*. Your goal is to hit the ball with your body turn, using your left hip joint to pivot your body around with no weight shift and no conscious effort to use your hands. It's a dead-arms shot in which the toe of the club head never turns over the heel as it does for a normal, full-power swing. When you hit the lob, you use the bounce of your sand wedge to slide under the ball. If you do it correctly, you'll get the height you need because the club face stays open and lofted.

■ The Lob Swing

Start your swing by simply turning your chest away from the target, so that everything moves away from the ball as a unit. Don't try to cock your wrists early; let them cock when and where they should, in response to the momentum of your club head and the swing of your arms. The same forces pull your shoulders around until your back faces the target. Because you have an open stance, it is imperative that you swing along your shoulder line and not "chase" the ball down the target line.

■ The Fall to the Ball

Your downswing is characterized by *the sweet surrender to gravity,* a phrase I use to emphasize the absence of manipulation as you allow your club head to fall to the ball—this means no lateral body motion and certainly no hitting with your hands. If you simply rotate your body around your left hip, your club head will move down your shoulder line to impact with a slightly open face, perfect for producing high, soft shots.

■ Pitching from a Thin Lie

Tight lies with not much grass under the ball can be a problem, but here's how to pitch the ball from a bald spot. Choose your sand wedge to give you the proper amount of loft. To guard against hitting it fat, place your weight in your front hip and stand closer to the ball so your club shaft is more vertical and your club head is on its toe, reducing the bounce of the club. This way you lessen the chance of snagging your club head because less of its surface is exposed to the ground. Your upright posture also causes you to raise your hands at address, protecting your wrists from overcocking.

Because the heel of your club is slightly off the ground, position the ball toward the toe of your club where you'll want to make contact. Striking the ball on the toe is not only safer, but the slightly off-center hit produces a much softer shot that allows you to swing more aggressively as a guard against quitting on the shot. Note that except for the reduced wrist action, once you're set up correctly, your swing is the same as it is for a normal pitch shot.

■ The Chip

When you chip, you change clubs the same way you do in your full swing, and with practice you'll be able to eyeball the distance and choose the right club, say a five-iron for a long running shot and a nine- for a short one. Pick a landing area about one yard onto the green where you want your chip to land. This way, every chip you hit flies a short distance, lands about one yard onto the green, then rolls to the hole like a putt. When you putt, you keep your body still and simply move your arms and shoulders with no wrist action, and it's the same with the short chip. As the distance increases there is a bit more body movement—just enough to allow a smooth stroke.

Position the ball off your back toe with the shaft vertical and inclined toward your front shoulder; your weight stays anchored on your front foot and you use only your arms and shoulders to move the club.

■ How to Chip in Detail

When you're around the green, get in the habit of asking two questions: One, can I use my putter? and two, if not, can I use a low-lofted club like a six- or seven-iron and chip it? Obviously you can't roll the ball when conditions prevent it—for example, the grass your ball must roll through is too long—but that's a judgment call, and your scores will reflect how well you make the call. The general rule, however, is if you can putt it, do so. The reason for this is that when you're hitting a ball to a target, it's easier to judge the distance if it's rolling versus trying to fly the ball most of the way to the cup. Basically the accuracy of your shot decreases as the height of the club head increases during the backswing, because the higher the club gets, the harder it is to return it correctly at impact.

It isn't a good idea to automatically reach for your wedge on short shots because you're introducing side spin. You won't know whether

Since you want the ball to spend most of its journey to the cup on the ground, choose the lowest-lofted iron that will carry onto the green about a yard or so and then roll the rest of the way like a putt. The triangle formed by your hands, arms, and shoulders at address will simply tilt down a bit on the backswing and then up during the downswing.

Note that the target shoulder is higher during the follow-through due to this seesaw motion. The stroke is made with little wrist break while keeping the weight on the front foot all the way through the stroke. The club head is low to the ground both on the backswing and the follow-through.

the ball is going to run, check up, or slow down then skid. The more loft you use the more inconsistent your chipping will be, so always use the least loft you can. Since the idea is to keep the ball on the ground for most of its journey, a properly executed chipping stroke with any club keeps the club head low to the ground. In keeping this predominantly horizontal path in relationship to the ground, you increase your chances of making dead-center contact at impact. The advantage of contacting the ball on the sweet spot of your club face is that solid contact minimizes the twisting of the club face, giving you an accurate roll in terms of distance and direction.

If you're not using your putter, your next choice would be the least-lofted club that will carry the ball onto the green about one or two paces and then run the rest of the way to the hole. To do this, keep your weight on your front side and make the stroke with minimal wrist cock. The proper chipping technique for the average player is a coordinated movement of the shoulders, arms, and hands that ensures that the butt of the club moves in the same direction as the face of the club until after the golf ball is hit. The most common error in chipping is to allow the target wrist to break down before impact, creating a situation where the butt of the club is moving in the opposite direction as the club face. This causes the club head to reach the bottom of the arc too soon before impact and results in either hitting behind the ball or making topped chips that roll much too far.

Image words create pictures on your mental screen. Since images cue motor responses, your golf vocabulary should have the appropriate image words to help you execute. The image word for the chip is *staccato,* which describes the firm action where you trap the ball against the ground. Most good chippers hold the club more firmly than in their regular swing, since they do not want their wrists to hinge very much during the stroke.

Position the ball off the toe of your trail foot with about 90 percent of your weight on your target foot. Your club face should sit square to the target with the shaft vertical and the heel slightly off the ground. Once the shaft is vertical, incline it until it points at your front shoulder. This sets your hands well ahead of the ball, ensuring the ball will be low and running. The execution is a one-piece, back-and-through stroke using only your arms and shoulders. The weight starts, stays, and finishes on the front foot.

Note that your wrists should remain firm so that your hands do not hinge or unhinge until after the ball is gone. Before you actually hit the shot take several practice swings and actually clip the grass. This will help you measure your distance to the ball. While not the only way to chip, I think this no-wrists method is the most forgiving of the chipping methods because it has fewer moving parts—it's simply straight back and through to the target.

■ Point and Chip

At the University of Rochester, Dana Ballard, a professor of computer science, is studying the science of visual optics by learning the intricacies of how human beings perceive visual depth and gather information that is then relayed to the motor cortex for execution. This skill is automatic, but understanding how your brain processes the information necessary to track your target can make you a better chipper. As Dr. Ballard discovered, the eye determines the distance and break to the hole by a series of "fixations," where the eye looks at and evaluates portions of the route your ball should take, one at a time. Information about your chip is stored in "working memory"—a very short-term brain function that lets you hold the information just long enough for it to be acted on. Basically all you have to do is point your eyes in the correct direction, pay attention to

Bob Murphy, master of the short game, practices his chipping by visualizing the arc of the chip. When you practice, combine the fundamentals of your setup with the visual data gathering that increases both your distance and direction control. Choose a chip that's on a flat part of the green and lay out three spots along its line (use something flat like the name tags from your golf bag). Then point your eyes at each section from near to far to gather information. Once you've done this, you're good to go.

what you're looking at, aim your club face and arrange your body, then put mechanics out of your mind.

■ *The Wood Chip and Run*

Lofting a sand wedge high in the air and stopping it close to the pin may be spectacular to watch, but it's not a high-percentage shot, especially if you've drawn a difficult lie. A good choice here is a fairway wood that you use like a putter, a shot made famous by Tiger Woods but one that has been used by Tour players such as Chi Chi Rodriguez for many years. It's especially effective when you have to play the shot up a slope to an elevated green because, instead of the ball rolling all the way along the ground, the loft of the three-wood causes the ball to hop into the air just after you hit it. This way it doesn't become snagged in the grass or knocked off line as it might if you chose a putter.

A fairway wood is an excellent choice, as it has enough loft to lift the ball out of difficult lies and its long shaft allows you a compact swing that's low to the ground. To chip with a wood, use either your putting or full-swing grip, assume a slightly open stance, and tilt the shaft of your club until it's upright. You'll have to stand erect to accommodate the length of the shaft but be careful to keep your weight anchored on your front foot so you don't sway as you make your stroke. Now use your putting stroke, keeping the trail wrist angle of address throughout the swing. Let your club head swing through the hitting zone as an extension of your arms so your club head "chases" the ball to the target.

The three-wood putt is also a good shot choice when your ball stops against the first cut of rough just off the green. It's hard to

When your ball lies just off the green and there's no obstacle between you and the pin that prevents you from rolling the ball, the play is a fairway wood.

judge this shot because using a normal chip or pitch, you're denied clean contact with the ball due to the intervening grass. The weight and mass of your three-wood head ensures that the club slides through the grass to contact the ball crisply. But be careful. Since your ball will have extra overspin on it you won't have to hit it as hard as you would a putt of the same length. How do you judge how hard to hit it? *Practice.*

The basic mechanics are as follows:

1 Weight on the front foot

2 Ball position off shirt logo

3 Use putting stroke with no wrist break

As you do in chipping, raise your three-wood on its toe, close the face, and grip down on it with your putting grip. Assume a narrow, open stance and stroke the ball as you would a putt.

CHAPTER 5

Putting

How to Hold Your Putter

If you want to be a good putter, you've got to produce the right combination of distance and direction, just as in the full swing. In order to do this you must accomplish two things: (1) Your putter must strike the ball with the appropriate force in the center of the club face with the putter head horizontal to the ground; and (2) your putter face needs to be looking directly down the intended line of roll. The grip depicted in the photos on page 113 will help you do this, and you can use this grip for both putting and chipping, since it encourages the firm-wristed stroke motion necessary for both types of shots.

Assuming that the greens you putt on are in decent shape, the stroke that I'd recommend is a back-and-forth pendulum action where the arc of the putter head is of equal length in both directions. Remember that pendulums swing from a central pivot point, and in putting your pivot point is located just under your throat. This point must not slide back and forth. It should remain a center around which your shoulders and arms swing the putter back and forth in

Lee Trevino uses a piston-type putting motion, where the right arm drives the stroke, as do many good putters. He creates a bend in his right wrist at address with the back of his left hand facing the target, and his goal with every putt is to keep this relationship intact as he makes his stroke. Note that even though he's already hit the putt, the butt of his club is still even with the club head showing that he kept the angle of his right wrist throughout his stroke while his right arm acted as a piston.

a rocking motion. Here's a tip that will make your stroke more consistent: Starting at address and continuing from start to finish, keep the space between your elbows the same. When you maintain the distance between your elbows (neither narrowing nor widening the gap between them), your putter head will always strike the ball at the exact bottom of its arc.

At address square your shoulders and hips to the target line. Then, bend forward from your hip sockets until your eyes are directly over the target line. Now, making sure that your eyes are still over the target line, rotate your head just enough to position your dominant eye directly over the ball. Position the putter shaft in the middle of your body with the ball directly in front of the putter face. To locate the target from this position, you need only rotate your head instead of disrupting your eye line by lifting your head but be sure to return your eyes back to their original position before you putt.

There are a myriad of ways to hold a putter, but if you're just starting out I'd stay with a few basics. Unlike your grip for your full swing, when you putt, position the handle of the putter in your palms rather than your fingers, as shown for the trail hand in photo (a). Once both hands are on the club, your palms face each other so that your hands work as a unit. This also means that the palm of your trail hand faces in the direction of the target, which encourages the putter head to move back and forth along the target line. Also make sure that both thumbs are on top of the grip to prevent your hands from twisting during your stroke. This allows the handle and the putter head to move together.

■ The Key to a Great Stroke

If there were a World Series of putting, where only skill with the flat stick counts, it wouldn't be surprising if the winner used an "unconventional" putting stroke. But I'll bet my one-iron that no matter who won and no matter what technique was used, the handle of the putter and the club face would arrive at the ball moving together in the direction of the target rather than the handle going one way and the club head another. The correct method preserves both the loft and the aim of the putter face through impact and,

Unlike the full swing, putting is an upper-body-oriented motion without any wrist action. Therefore, the grip and stance are very different from the ones you use on your full swing. Start by placing the right side of the grip against the lifeline of your right hand, as I have done in photo (a), then rest your right thumb on the top side of the putter grip. In the same manner, place the left side of the grip against the lifeline of your left hand and put your left thumb on the top side of the putter grip. The finished product should look like my grip in photo (b) with the right palm, the back of your left hand, and the putter face all pointing in the same direction. In order to roll the ball accurately, you should keep all these relationships throughout your putting stroke without any wrist action. Notice I have wrapped my left index finger over the fingers of my right hand. This is called a reverse overlap grip, and it also helps to quiet your wrists.

DOMINANT EYE AND GOOD PUTTING

Since your visual system is a strong determiner of how your muscles move, your putting stroke will follow your eye alignment—in essence, you putt where you look. Thus how you position your eyes at address affects where you'll think the hole is. With your eyes outside your target line, you'll see the hole as being left of where it really is and you'll miss a well-stroked putt to the left. With your eyes inside the target line, you'll misaim to the right, leaving a correctly putted ball to the right of the cup. When you misaim both your eyes and your putter head, the only chance you have to hole the putt is to make a bad putting stroke, and this is not the way to become a good putter.

Here are two essentials for correct eye alignment:

1. An imaginary line connecting your eyes should be directly over the target line at address.
2. Your dominant eye should be directly over the ball.

You can determine your "eye dominance" as follows:

1. With both eyes open, look at an object about 20 feet away.
2. Raise a finger and line it up so that your finger is overlapping the object.
3. Now close one eye. If it looks like your finger "jumped" and it is no longer in line with the object, then the eye you closed is "dominant."

assuming that your aim was correct in the first place, sends the ball rolling down the target line.

If you're having trouble keeping your putts on line, you're probably letting your target arm stop just before impact. When this happens, your trail wrist releases its angle and your target wrist cups so your knuckles fold toward your front forearm, causing the butt of your club to move in the opposite direction of the club face. "Slapping" your putts changes the face angle your putter had at address, producing side spin that causes your ball to wobble off line.

You may be a "pop" putter like Arnold Palmer was in his champion years—the handle and face arrive at impact moving in the same direction and then the face passes the handle. Or you could be a firm-wristed "stroke" putter such as Phil Mickelson, who uses only his shoulders and arms so that the handle and face stay together for a short way after impact as the club head rises above the ground. It makes no difference. In both styles, the putter handle and club face arrive at impact moving in the same direction.

Try the following test to see if your putting problems are the result of your club head passing your hands at impact. Mark five balls with a stripe around the middle and place the stripe perpendicular to the ground. If the stripe rolls end over end during your ball's roll to the hole, you're making solid contact. If the stripe wobbles as the ball rolls, your wrists are breaking down through impact.

To learn how to keep the butt of your club moving with the club face, plant a shaft in the ground at a 45-degree angle just outside your front foot. Put a head cover on the top of the shaft so you don't scratch your hand. Set at the correct angle, the shaft should extend onto the path your hands would travel during your follow-through. Now stroke a few putts, making sure to keep your target arm moving through contact. Your target hand should meet the shaft at the same time your putter head passes beneath it. Done correctly, you should be able to both see and feel a correct stroke.

As good a player as Tom Weiskopf was, he made the mistake of letting his left wrist break down through impact, causing the putter to flip over.

The ball will roll truer and the solidness of contact will produce a "soft" feeling in your hands as you contact the ball with the sweet spot of your club face.

Putting is a game of direction and distance, and until you correctly line up and consistently hit the ball on the sweet spot of the putter, you will never receive the correct feedback from your putts that will allow you to improve. So spend time practicing these fundamentals—there's no faster way to lower your handicap. Good putting can save you when your full swing lets you down.

■ *Top This!*

The most accurate stroke in golf is one that is as level as possible to the ground, because a level stroke preserves the true loft of the

INSIDER GOLF'S TOP ELEVEN TIPS FOR READING PUTTS

1. When reading a putt, you should look at your line from three vantage points: (1) from behind the hole, looking back toward your ball; (2) from the low side of the line, looking into the break; and (3) from behind the ball, looking back toward the hole. Unless you've determined that the putt is dead straight, this final view will not be on a straight line drawn from the hole to the ball—you will be standing on the arc or curve of the ball's projected line.

2. It is as a putt approaches the hole and starts slowing in speed that it becomes most susceptible to slope and will break the most. So pay particular attention to the area around the hole to determine the ball's final approach line to the hole.

3. If in doubt as to which direction a putt breaks, assume that it is a straight putt.

4. On all putts, first establish the line, then concentrate on producing the correct distance.

5. When reading your putt, visualize how water would run off the green during a heavy rainfall. Architects build courses so that water won't puddle on the greens. If you can figure the drainage patterns, you'll make a much better read, because slope has the most effect on your putt of any of the variables.

6. As golfers bend to extract the ball from the hole, rather than step on the hole itself they step all around it. So the ground around the cup becomes recessed, and the cup itself raised. This crowning is too slight to see with the human eye, but putts that approach this crown at too slow a speed are deflected away from the hole. To prevent this, especially late in the day, you should ram your short putts into the cup.

7. Adjust your speed according to the time of day. Greens tend to be slow in the morning, when dew and irrigation moisture are present. They get faster in the late morning and early afternoon as the sun dries them out, and then slow down again at dusk, when the grass is longer and evening moisture returns.

8. Know your grass. Bent-grass greens tend to be faster with less grain than Bermuda greens.

9. Putts tend to break *away* from greenside bunkers by design because architects build slopes that prevent water draining into them. So find the bunkers when you putt.

10. Know the direction of your grain. If the green appears to be shiny, you're downgrain, and the putt will be faster than it appears. If it's dull in color, you are going into the grain and need to hit it harder.

11. Make your final read while standing on the curve or arc of your putt—it will give your brain the most accurate images to produce a successful putt.

club giving you a much better chance of a square club face at impact. It's the level club head and minimal verticality that makes the putter a good choice for this trouble shot. You may only use this shot twice a year, but you should have it in your arsenal—and it can be quite a conversation piece after the round.

Let's set the stage: You're in the rough just short of the green and you're in the middle of a deep divot with a steep front lip left by someone who used a wedge to loft the ball to the pin. The flag is at the back of the green and there are no hazards in your way.

As crazy as it looks, with a little creativity you can putt out of this situation, and if you know how, it's the best shot to play. In photo (a) I'm set up so I hit the top of the ball creating overspin that will be increased when the ball hits the lip of the divot. Note that I hover the putter so it points at the top part of the ball, exactly where I want to make contact. I'm visualizing a level stroke that sends the ball spinning off the lip of the divot and rolling to the pin.

Photo (b), on the right, shows that it's not a wristy stroke—my right arm is still in line with the shaft, indicating that I've used my chest and arm rather than my hands to make this shot happen.

Nothing should prevent you from rolling the ball except that, from the middle of the divot, it's almost impossible to make clean contact—unless you hit the top of the ball so that your ball caroms off the lip of the divot, pops up into the air, and hits the green with an abundance of overspin that carries it to the flag. Begin by hovering your putter head behind the ball, even with the top third of the ball. From this position simply make a level arm-and-shoulder stroke with no independent wrist action.

■ *Which Putter for You?*

When you're scheduled to play a course where there is a lot of grain, your putting touch will determine your success. Consider carrying two putters. Use a lightweight blade putter for the lightning-fast, downgrain, downslope attempts. Your lighter downhill blade putter allows you to stroke rather than punch your quicker putts. Use a heavy putter to help get the ball rolling against the grain and up the steep slopes. A centered shaft might help prevent the club head from twisting on firm putts.

Basically, putters are designed to get the ball rolling, rather than hopping or bouncing. Because putting surfaces vary in both texture and speed, a wide range of putting designs are available. On slow, wet greens, you want a heavy putter with plenty of loft to help the ball skip a little before it goes into its roll. This extra loft also helps on extremely grainy greens. If you are playing fast, closely mown surfaces, a light putter with less loft will get the ball rolling its truest.

■ *Left-Hand Low Putting Can Help*

First, setting up with the grip shown in the photos on page 113 allows you to have your shoulders level at address, making it easier to control the back-and-through pendulum action of your stroke with the big muscles of the back and shoulders rather than the smaller muscles of your hands and arms.

Second, the solid position of your left hand (right for left-handers) and wrist throughout the stroke helps avoid the most common fault in putting—the left wrist collapse. Clearly, if the relationship of the back of the left hand and the putter face are compromised through impact you can pull the ball to the left or push it to the right. But with your left hand low, it's easier to feel that your left wrist and the putter face mirror each other through the ball; it's also easier to keep your right hand bent at the same angle through-out the stroke. It's a one-lever stroke from your left shoulder right through the putter head.

Third, as you study my stroke from the top of my back stroke to the end of my follow-through, notice how my putter head is low to the ground. Placing my left hand below my right promotes this and keeps the stroke on line longer, which is always a good trait.

How to Practice Your Putting

In putting you need to get two things right—the speed (distance) and the direction. Here is a way to develop the proper speed on your putt. Mark off six-, 15-, and 30-foot putts on the practice green. Assume your address position with your feet perpendicular to the line you want the ball to start on, and position the ball in the mid-dle of your feet. Starting with the 30-footer, make a practice stroke and notice the length of your backswing. Next, spread your stance by moving your right foot back to the point where your backswing ended. Now adjust your front foot so the ball is still in the middle of your stance. Stroke the putt by taking the putter back to your back foot (big toe) and through to your front foot the same distance on the follow-through.

Do this for the three distances until you develop a feel for how much backswing you need for each length of putt, then practice putting toe to toe, focusing only on producing the correct distance.

■ *Are There "Nots" in Your Putting?*

For an enlightening experience go to any practice putting green and watch golfers putt. In actuality what you'll see is golfers practicing

Start by taking a normal putting grip with your right hand: palm square to the putter face, the putter grip running diagonally through the palm along the lifeline, and the right thumb sitting gently on top. Then place your left hand below your right with the back of the hand square to the putter face and wrap your fingers snugly into position. This "left-hand low" or "reverse-handed" putting grip can help you satisfy several desirable putting principles.

missing putts! It goes something like this: They throw down five balls and from 15 feet they leave the first putt short, pull the next two, push the fourth, and crash the fifth attempt 10 feet by the hole. And it's not long before the brain gets the message—"I'm *not* going to make many putts today." Thus the golfer goes to the course perfectly prepared to miss everything but the gimmees and the knock-aways.

Statistics show that on average a Tour player misses about 50 percent of the six-foot putts he attempts over the course of a year. And that's on perfect greens! So what chance does a weekend golfer have from 15 feet on bumpy, overused practice greens, where the cup rotation is not daily. Keep track of how many putts you make in a putting session and I'll bet you it's less than 20 percent.

You can change this around simply by following these guidelines:

1 Spend most of your practice time getting the correct distance on your putts. If by some magic (or some practice) you always had the right distance on your putts, you'd be a heck of a putter. Most three-putts occur because of poor distance, not bad direction. Look at it this way: Unless there's a huge, slippery break, it's hard to miss a putt left or right by six feet but it's easy to leave one six feet short or long.

To develop your touch for distance, lay out three shafts on the putting green at intervals of 10, 20, and 30 feet. Then drop three balls and putt to the shafts. First putt all three balls to the same shaft. Next stroke a ball to the 30-foot shaft, then the next ball to the 20-foot, and the last to the 10-foot. Then change the intervals between the shafts. The good thing here is that you may have putted long or short of your shaft but you haven't "missed" in the traditional sense and since you haven't seen a ball *not* go in, there's no *nots* in your putting.

2 Finish up by seeing the putts go in the hole. Just before you end your session find a level three-footer and ram four or five putts dead center into the middle of the cup. Then go play golf knowing that you can putt up to three feet from anywhere and make it.

■ Gimme a Break: Why Most Golfers Finish on the Low Side

The target line is an imaginary straight line between the target and your ball, useful for a putt that's dead straight but not so for putts that have some break to them. The problem is that on breaking putts, if the cup is your target, the tendency is either to push putts that break left to right or pull those that curve right to left because the face of the putter instinctively turns so that it faces towards the hole at impact. Unfortunately this starts the ball at the hole without allowing for any break, so the ball finishes on the low side of the hole assuming the speed is correct. It is because of this club face manipulation during the stroke that most golfers miss on the low side even though they tell themselves before the stroke to allow for enough break.

THE BREAK POINT

On breaking putts, you should putt to the break point instead of the cup. Once you have determined where the putt is going to begin the major portion of its break to the hole, that should be your new target. If you focus on the hole you'll either push or pull the putt because you'll subconsciously try to roll it to the hole on the target line. To practice using the break point, mark it with a flat object and focus on rolling your ball over that mark.

The best way to stop pulling and pushing your putts is to forget about the hole and focus on the break point. Here's how: Read the break, then pick a spot on the curve or arc of the putt where the putt will start the major portion of its break to the hole. Once this spot is selected it takes the place of the hole as your target. Then, having lined your putter face up with that spot, forget about direction (it's taken care of at address) and focus on producing the correct speed that will send the ball rolling along the arc and breaking to the hole at just the right point.

Once you know the amount of curve on the putt, you need to get your brain used to putting to a spot on the arc of the putt rather than the final destination—the hole. To do this, mark your break point with an object like a coin and practice rolling your ball over it.

Here are two keys to reading the curve of the putt:

1 Always start your line-up from behind the ball to allow your eyes to take pictures of the break. Then approach the ball, set your putter face behind it in the direction you want the ball to start and align your body perpendicular to the putter face.

2 When you line up the putt, you should position yourself behind the ball on that part of the arc of the putt that extends behind the ball. Too many players try to line up a curved putt by standing on a straight line to the cup.

TRIANGULATION: All You Have to Pay Is *Attention*

Make sure you have a putting routine designed to locate the target by gathering the information about distance and direction necessary to get the ball in the hole. Your brain is an expert at tracking objects, and all it needs is information to tell you exactly where the cup is, data that many golfers fail to provide when it comes time to read a putt. They're depriving their brain of its need-to-know info, and you can't do that if you want to be a good putter.

The method that will help you gather the information you need is called *triangulation,* where you look at your putt from three vantage points. When you use just one position to determine the location of the cup you're likely to encounter parallax—distortion via the position of the observer. That's why surveyors use more than one position to measure the exact location of objects. They can't afford to be fooled and neither can you.

The three positions match points on the triangle:

1 from behind the hole (temporary commitment one)

2 from midway to the hole, on the low side (temporary commitment two)

3 from behind the ball (final commitment)

As you move from point to point on the triangle, your commitment to the line of the putt often changes. This is as it should be because, as you gather more information from different vantage points, your brain adjusts the line or curve of the putt *automatically.* For your brain to do its thing, the only thing you have to pay is attention.

As you gather information from behind and on the low side of the hole, your commitment to the line of your putt is temporary because as you study your line from different angles, you may change your mind. But when you go behind the ball, you make a final commitment and it stays with you through your entire stroke. It's called "triangulation," and its goal is to give your brain enough information to generate this final commitment.

CHAPTER 6

Sand Play

Splash It Out

In the sand around the green, your club never directly contacts the ball, so the ball rides out of the bunker on a cushion or splash of sand. Your sand wedge has bounce, a bulge on the bottom of the club head designed to avoid catching in the sand, which allows your club to skim rather than dig. A correctly hit splash shot sounds like a *poof* rather than a thud.

Splash Mechanics

Open your stance by drawing your front foot away from your target line enough to re-aim your club face back at the target (aim your club face directly at the target, but be careful not to touch the sand with your club head because that's a penalty). Dig your feet into the sand for stability. This lowers your feet in relationship to the level of the ball, guaranteeing that you'll hit the sand first, a

The photos show why it's called a splash shot—the club head doesn't dig, it *splashes* into the sand just behind the ball. Note the early and aggressive cocking of the wrists. Note also that the golfer takes some sand hitting about an inch or so behind the ball but not nearly as much as the high handicapper, who usually hits too far behind the ball.

necessary feature of the splash shot. But be careful to stand slightly farther from the ball because when you dig your feet in, you move the hosel of the club closer to the ball. The guideline is that for every inch you dig in, move back an inch. Position your weight on your front foot and leave it there throughout your swing. You won't need the power a weight transfer would produce, so be sure to leave the pressure in your front leg throughout your motion. Let your arms and shoulders move the club back along your toe line and then simply continue this rotation back to the ball ending in a high finish.

To do this correctly you'll need to slice across the ball, so move the ball forward in your stance opposite your front heel. You'll also need to open the face of your club so it points directly at your target. When you open your stance be sure to let your hips and shoulders open too. This sets your entire body in a position that allows you to swing your club along your body line as represented by your toe line—a cutting action that puts side spin on the ball.

THE BOARD OF EDUCATION

Too many golfers think they have to dig into the sand to hit the ball out of the bunker, but this faulty concept causes them to take too much sand, leaving the ball either in the bunker or way short of the pin. The greenside bunker shot from a decent lie is a *splash not a bash*. Everything you do in your setup and swing is directed toward letting the bounce on your sand wedge slide through the sand and under the ball, creating a *poof* sound as the club head slides along the sand rather than the thud of a club head that buries in the sand.

To feel the correct motion of the splash shot, bury a board in the sand and take a few practice swings to get the feeling of your club head bouncing rather than digging. Then place a ball on the sand next to the board and reproduce the "splash" feeling while hitting a sand shot from a normal lie. If you have trouble, go back to the board until you can hit the splash shot correctly every time.

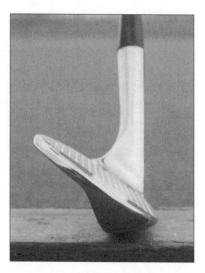

Because of the flange on the club, when it sits correctly, its leading edge is off the ground.

About Your Sand Wedge

Some special features of your sand wedge make it your best choice in a greenside bunker, but a sand wedge is often a good choice in other greenside situations, like from deep rough or pitching to a tight pin. Since it's the heaviest club in your bag, it cuts through thick rough much easier than your other clubs. It also has the most loft, ranging anywhere from 56 to 60-plus degrees (the lob wedge), so it's ideal for producing the high, soft shot you need to carry over a bunker.

The Bash Technique

You'll use the leading edge of your sand wedge to bury in the sand for the bash technique, so make sure that your club face is a square position (not open, like for the splash). To do this, play it back of

When your ball is sitting down in the sand, there's only one way to get it out—
take your medicine and *blast* it somewhere onto the green. In this case you want
the club head to dig, so there's not much of a follow-through.

center toward your target foot. The weight starts, stays, and finishes
on the front hip, but unlike a regular sand shot where you open your
shoulders, keep your shoulders square to your *target line* as you open
your stance. This distribution will make you feel tilted slightly forward with your head, and your weight is ahead of the ball.

As your club swings back to the ball allow your club head to de-
scend to the ball at a steep angle with little or no follow-through.
The trick is to hit down into the sand to make the ball pop out; if
you try to help the ball out with a lifting motion the ball will stay
in the bunker.

Another factor to consider is the makeup of the sand. Thick, wet sand is no place for the bash technique. Wet sand transmits energy to the ball very efficiently, so that you can use the smooth, easy-does-it-swing-style of the splash shot. It's just the opposite when you're faced with dry, heavy beach sand that absorbs the blow, forcing you to dig your ball out with the bash technique.

The Fairway Bunker Shot

If there's one shot that worries the average golfer more than a short bunker shot, it's a long one. But unless you're in a deep pit, most fairway bunkers are quite negotiable if you use the proper technique. Let's say you're in a fairway bunker about 150 yards from the green. Here your goal is to catch the ball cleanly, by picking it from the sand. To do this, assume an open stance with your front shoulder pointing about 25 degrees wide of the target. Position the ball even with the left side of your face to promote a swing that is level with the sand through the hitting area.

Select one more club than normal and set 60 percent of your weight on your front foot. You want to establish firm footing, but don't dig your feet way down in the sand as you would for a greenside-bunker shot because it places your body on a level lower than the ball and that's a sure way to hit the sand first—just the opposite of what you're trying to do.

The trick to hitting solid shots from fairway bunkers is to make a full chest turn away from the ball, without letting your weight transfer to your back foot, as you would out of the grass. By keeping the 60-40 distribution throughout your swing, you neutralize the adverse footing and give yourself a solid lower body platform from which to catch the ball cleanly.

Play the ball in the middle of your stance. Take care not to dig your feet into the sand as you would in a normal greenside bunker; this would increase your chances of catching the ball heavy. During the downswing, take care to keep your spine angle so there's no chance of dropping your body down toward the ball. While a thin shot is okay here, fat is not. Also notice the full follow-through.

Neither Splash Nor Bash:
The Chip From Greenside Bunker

Part of being a skillful player is reading the situation, choosing the right shot, and then being able to execute the shot. Knowing your options is important, but most golfers never consider the chip from a greenside sand bunker as a viable shot. Part of the reason is they don't often see the pros do it because they stay with the explosion shot.

This low tolerance for error makes the sand chip one of the toughest of the awkward shots, which is why the preferred technique in the sand bunker involves hitting the sand behind the ball so the

When you chip out of the bunker, you must catch the ball first just as you would for a chip shot that isn't sand-bound. This makes it a dangerous shot because the margin for error is so small—catch just a waif of sand before you make contact with the ball and the shot is ruined.

ball comes out on a cushion of sand. As you are probably well aware, when you hit a normal sand shot, you actually hit the ball "fat" on purpose so there is always sand between your club face and the ball, meaning that you never really hit the ball directly with the face of your club. Not so with the sand chip, where the goal is to pick the ball cleanly from the sand.

Here's how:

The object of chipping from the bunker is to produce a low shot that lands on the green and rolls to the hole like a putt. Choose this shot only when there is very little lip on the bunker. Since your ball rolls like a putt you can study the break and play for it; the break is something that's hard to judge with the explosion technique unless you're a good bunker player. One advantage of the sand chip is that if you pull it off, it's almost as accurate as putting—something that can't be said for blasting out of the sand.

■ *Technique*

To chip the ball accurately from the sand, use your putting stroke with your putting grip (unless you putt cross-handed—then use your full swing grip). Your goal is twofold: minimize the possibility of wrist action, the great destroyer of the putting-chipping motion, and select an iron according to the length of roll you need. You might use a nine-iron for a short shot (say 15 feet), and a six-iron for a very long roll (say 50 feet)—but as a rule of thumb, use no iron below a five-.

Raise your iron on its toe so it's upright like your putter. Grip down on your iron to make it the same length as your putter. This moves you closer to the ball with your eyes over the target line as in putting. Position your weight on your front foot to promote a descending motion, then use the iron just like you do your putter, making a pendulum motion that's controlled by your upper body, with no lower body and no wrist action.

Here are two special keys for the shot:

1 Play the ball back of the center of your feet, with the butt of your club opposite your front thigh.

2 Take sand *after* you hit the ball, not before as you do with a normal sand shot.

Once these adjustments are in place simply execute your putting stroke.

CHAPTER 7

And One More Thing

Here are a few things more that are good for your game.

It Could Be the Arrows, Not the Indian

No matter what those infomercials pretend, you know as well as I that having the right clubs won't turn a 25-handicapper into a par golfer, but the right equipment can shave strokes off your score and help your swing develop. Clubs that fit you allow you to make your best possible golf swing and—here's the key—repeat that swing time after time.

The problem with ill-fitting equipment is that you have to make compensations in your swing, and inadvertently, you force yourself into a swing error to compensate for a misfit club—it's not a faulty club, it just doesn't fit you. But when your equipment is matched to your individual needs it becomes a complement to your swing, freeing you to perform to your true potential. The best way to do this is to find a PGA or an LPGA teaching professional who is skilled in club fitting. Your pro will take some static measurements indoors and then take you out to the range to measure your actual swing. You'll be given a variety of clubs to try while the teacher/club fitter evaluates how the club affects your swing and your ball flight.

One specification that has a major effect on the accuracy of your shots is the lie of the club.

■ Lie

All clubs are built with the toe slightly in the air to account for the in-swing bending of the shaft toward the ground. Lie is the angle that the shaft is drilled into the neck of the club, and when you have the wrong lies, the ball will not go where you're aiming. In this situation you have to make a bad swing to hit a good shot. If your swing is sound and your aim true, but you're still troubled by off-line shots, you should have your lies checked.

■ Flat and Upright

When you set up to the ball with good posture and the toe of your club is too much off the ground, your club face actually aims to the left of the target, so you'll need to bend your clubs to lower the toe. If the heel is up in the air when you're in a good address position, your club face aims to the right, so you'll need to bend them to lower the heel.

Most golf professionals have access to a machine that adjusts clubs to the proper lie angle by bending the shaft near the neck of your club. To test the lie, your golf professional or club fitter will put a piece of tape on the sole of your club and have you hit balls from what's known as a lie board. If the lie angle is correct for you, the tape will be marked in the center of the sole from its contact with the board; if the lie is incorrect, the evidence will be on the tape.

Maximizing Your Distance:
Invitation to a Power Launch

It used to be thought that swing speed was the big determiner of how far you hit the ball, but scientists now tell us that while it's part of the story, it's not that simple. You must address three parameters: If you can increase your launch angle, increase the ball speed as it leaves the club face, and decrease the spin rate of your ball, you'll hit it farther.

Golf Magazine reports that the average player's ball comes off the club face at about nine degrees, spinning at 3,700 revolutions per minute, whereas PGA Tour players launch it at more than 11 degrees and about 2,200 rpm; the drive for dough boys like long-drive champ Jason Zuback launch at 13 degrees and 1,800 rpm.

Here are a few things you can try to get your spin rate down and your launch angle up. Keep in mind that they may not work for you if you have some glaring swing errors. If this is the case, see your PGA pro and get your swing fixed before you do anything else.

■ *Setup Changes*

Try the simplest first—move the ball forward two inches and tee it higher than you ever have. You'll determine how much by experiment. This may not work if you have a slow swing speed, but I'd give it a try if you're average or above. Chi Chi Rodriguez used to tee it on a pencil and later taped two tees together so he would be sure to catch the ball on the upswing, and in his prime he was the longest hitter pound for pound on the Tour.

■ *Equipment*

Experiment with a more flexible-shafted, deep-faced driver with a low kick point. It may well give you a catapult effect where the ball leaps off the club face with higher velocity and less spin.

Everything else being equal, the longer the shaft, the higher the club-head speed, so if you lengthen your driver, your initial velocity off the face will increase. Jarmo Sandelin on the European Tour and Rocky Thompson on the Senior Tour have drivers that are 50 inches long, but too much of a good thing becomes a bad thing. Most golfers shouldn't go over 46 inches because of the tendency to miss the sweet spot—and that costs you yardage!

■ The Swing Itself

The best change you can make in your swing that will maximize your launch conditions is to hit the ball solidly, which is a little like saying that to improve your financial condition you need more money. But there is one all-purpose salve that can help, and that's to improve your tempo. Try hovering the club at address (instead of resting on the ground behind the ball) and then counting rhythmically as you swing—one for the backswing; two for the downswing; and three for the finish.

■ Awkward Lies

Ben Hogan said that "golf is a game of adjustments," but you'd never know it by the way most people practice. They look for level lies on the driving range with perfect grass—and unfortunately that's not what happens when you get to the course. If you've played any golf at all, you know that there are situations on the course where the ball is either above or below your feet, and if you don't make the necessary adjustments, uneven lies can ruin your round.

There are four basic types of uneven lies: (1) ball above your feet, (2) ball below your feet, (3) downhill, and (4) uphill. For each of these, you must make several adjustments to compensate for the effect of the hill's slope.

Ball Below Feet

When the ball is below your feet, your swing is upright (more up-and-down than it is around) because you must stand closer to the ball. With a more upright swing, your club face tends to be open when you strike the ball, producing a shot that's lower with a cut spin on it—left to right for the right-hander. If the better player makes a mistake from this lie it usually is a pull, while the average golfer will no doubt hit a low slice.

At address notice how this player's knees are turned in. This gives her a stable platform on a slope where it would be easy to lose her balance. While her swing is primarily upper body–oriented, there is still a transfer of weight to her front leg during the downswing as is evident in the second photo. Note how her ponytail hangs pretty much in the same position in both frames—that's because she kept her head quiet and drove her right shoulder through the ball.

Set the club in place behind the ball before you take your stance so that the shaft of your club is more upright than normal. Although you don't try to do it, the vertical shaft adjusts the club so the heel is off the ground—this aims the club face to the right of the target (for the right-hander). It's best to move the ball forward in your stance. This will allow you to catch the ball solidly and give your club face time to square up to the target. Remember that since the ball is farther from you, the bottom of your arc will occur later in your swing, and that's where the ball should be when your club arrives. This forward ball position opens your shoulders to the target and encourages a slight pull that offsets the tendency for the ball to fly to the right because of the slope.

As you stand closer to the ball, widen your stance and increase your knee flex, a move that will lower you down the slope so you can better reach the ball. In addition turn both knees in as if you were knock-kneed, and pigeon-toe your feet. This will give you a stable lower platform that will prevent you from falling down the hill as you swing. Also be sure to anchor yourself so the weight distribution favors your heels as you sit down into the hill. One of the toughest things about this shot is to stay in the seated position during your swing because the slope will try to pull you forward onto your toes. Therefore, take care to stay "sitting" until after impact.

Downhill Lie

When your ball is on a slope, the first order of business is to maintain your balance. The definition of a pure downhill lie describes the ball as below your back foot and above your front. The problem here is making a good weight shift, because as the angle of the slope increases it becomes harder to shift your weight up the slope into your trail hip joint and even harder to stay behind the ball on the downswing since you never coiled behind the ball in the first

To handle the downhill lie, choose a more lofted club and position the ball to the middle of your stance. Tilt your shoulders to match the slope until your front shoulder is even with your back. Close your stance to level your hips and make a three-quarter motion, concentrating on keeping your balance throughout the swing. Don't try for a high finish—your hands should be about shoulder height or lower.

place. All of these circumstances conspire against you, causing you to hit low snipes to the right of the target.

Probably the biggest mistake golfers make in the downhill setup occurs when they set their shoulders as they normally do for a level lie—that is, front shoulder higher than back shoulder. Good players know you must tilt your shoulders down the hill so they match the slope of the hill as much as possible, even if the back shoulder is higher than the front on severe slopes.

Anchor your weight in your front hip, then resolve that even though you don't make a shift to your back hip, you definitely make an upper body turn away from the ball. This turn with no shift will give you stability plus coil on the tricky slope. The major error here is to try to lift the ball into the air, especially if the green is above your feet, so make sure to swing down the hill, letting your club head chase the contour of the slope.

To get the lay of the land, take your setup by anchoring your feet into the hill, and then swing your club head over the ball to determine what will happen to your balance. Make your practice swings as real as possible, except of course that your club head swings over the ball instead of actually hitting it. Once you know how the slope will affect your balance, make the following adjustments: Aim to the left of the target and draw your rear foot back until you level your hips. This not only provides you with stability but squares your shoulders to the target line. And be careful with your club choice—use *less* club (you might use a six-iron instead of a five-).

To ensure that you will make contact with the ball at the bottom of your swing arc play the ball in the middle of your stance. Turn your target foot in a bit as a brace to hit against at impact, and don't be afraid to continue down the hill as you start your follow-through. On a steep downhill slope you'll often see Tour players who look like they're walking after the ball on their follow-through. That's because they swing down the slope with their club head and step over their front leg as they "walk through" the shot. They look like they've lost their balance, but actually they've maintained it by letting the walk-through happen—and so should you.

Ball Above Feet

When the ball is above your feet, you're forced to swing more around yourself on a flatter arc, so the tendency is for the shot to go to the left—often with a hook spin. The adjustments you need to make are as follows.

Balance is your first concern on any shot, especially when you've drawn an awkward lie. Your goal is to neutralize the tendency to be pulled down the hill. Flex your knees into the hill with your weight forward toward the balls of your feet and leave it there as

To stay in control of her balance, this player sets her weight into the slope with a little more knee flex then usual. Look how low the shaft is—this means that her finish will be low and more around her. This is a tough shot, and our young golfer has everything under control—except her hair.

you swing. To prevent the momentum of your turn from forcing you down the hill, be sure to keep your weight on the inside rim of your back foot, just back of the middle of your stance. Choose at least one more club and choke down so you can stand closer to the ball. Close your shoulders to balance the tendency to pull the shot; this will automatically aim your club face to the right of the target. Once you set up like this the swing takes an inside path that offsets the tendency for the ball to start left. Having aimed properly, simply make a three-quarter swing, making sure that even though you've shortened your swing you haven't cheated yourself on coil. To do this, keep a bit more weight on your left side and let your hips resist your shoulder turn.

The Uphill Lie

When the ball is lower than your front foot but higher than your back foot, you've got yourself an uphill lie where the shot will have a higher trajectory than normal because the incline of the hill acts like a launching pad. Another aspect of the lie that adds height to your shot occurs when you sole your club behind the ball, effectively increasing the loft of the club face because of the slope.

Because the ball will fly higher than normal, you need to take more club from an uphill lie. If you normally hit a six- take the five-. Another adjustment you need to make stems from the tendency for your ball to fly to the left (for right-handers), but the adjustment is a simple one—just aim to the right of target. How much? That's where talent and experience come in.

When one foot is higher than the other it unlevels the hips—an awkward situation that makes it difficult to make solid contact. The solution is to play the ball from the middle of your stance and open your front shoulder and hip until your hips are level.

Don't forget to flare your front foot a few extra degrees to make it easier to turn your hips through the shot. Since you want to swing up the slope (not into it), tilt your shoulders to match the slope of the hill so your target shoulder is higher than your back shoulder. Anchor your weight on the inside rim of your back foot so that you're ready for what will occur at the top of your swing—namely, the momentum of your backswing will force you down the hill unless you've established your brace at address.

Even though there is very little weight shift during your backswing (the weight is already on your right side), there is a shift to your left side on the way back to the wall. The key to a good swing is to let your arm swing follow the slope of the hill so that you finish with your hands high and behind your target ear. It's possible that the momentum of your arm swing during your finish might even pull you backward down the hill. This is natural, so don't fight it— just be prepared to let it happen. In fact, it's a good idea on steep slopes to take a practice swing complete with a fall back down the hill at the finish.

Once you've made the correct adjustments in your setup, you need to do only two things: the first is to make a smooth, three-quarter swing for maximum control and the second is to focus on the target.

Fit For Golf: A Touch of Realism

If you're like most golfers, you're not going to put in a lot of gym time, even if it's good for your golf game. My advice is that rather than launching into an intense, time-consuming workout program that you'll abandon in a few weeks, start slow with a realistic program you know you can complete. You can always step it up later.

There are just a few basic things to remember.

- A muscle pulls in only one direction when it contracts, so in many instances there must be at least two groups (called antagonistic) to provide a full range of movement.

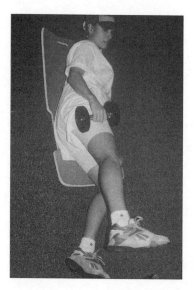

LPGA Tour star Michelle McGann visits the workout room to increase her leg drive.

- To keep yourself in balance, take care to always exercise both muscles in the antagonistic pair.

- You build *speed* by doing speed movements such as swinging a shaft with no club head on it as fast as you can. You build *strength* by weight training. To receive the benefit of both speed and strength, keep a shaft handy and swing it for speed after every heavy lift.

- Take the time to make an honest strength-weakness profile, and then allocate your workout accordingly. If you're very strong but inflexible, work on your flexibility. If you're as thin as a scarecrow, spend time lifting weights. If you're strong and flexible, maintain it and improve your cardiovascular fitness. If you're weak and inflexible, you need it all.

- For best results, work out three days a week with forty-eight hours layoff between each workout.

- Before you start this or any program consult your doctor.

The muscles selected below are geared to a workout for golf that takes less than forty minutes. If you have limited time and want to hit the most important golf muscles, here are the ones I'd choose.

■ *Hamstrings/Quadriceps*

They provide stabilization in your golf swing. Many golfers have weak hamstrings (muscles on the back of the upper leg that flex the leg) and therefore have trouble holding the flex in their legs as they swing.

■ *Triceps/Biceps*

The triceps extend your arms, while the biceps flex them. Your triceps help you to sling the club into the ball. Your right bicep folds the club during the backswing and your left stabilizes the club during your downswing.

■ *Pecs/Lats*

Your pectorals and latissimus dorsi are big muscles on your chest and back that play a huge role in your golf swing. The left lat helps rotate your left arm counterclockwise, moving it down and across your chest during your downswing, while the left pec moves your left arm in the opposite direction, toward the midline of your body. Your left lat pulls the club down, while the role of the left pec in the downswing is to put the brakes on the left arm, slowing it down as it approaches the hitting area so that energy can be delivered down the shaft and into the ball.

■ Hands/Forearms

You can strengthen your hands and forearms by squeezing a soft, palm-sized rubber ball. The hands and forearms are clamps that secure the club to the body. I have never seen a good player with weak forearms.

Kelly Blackburn has been developing specialized fitness programs to help individuals achieve their fitness goals. Since 1994, she has specialized in developing golf-specific training programs for both PGA Tour professionals and amateurs. The specific techniques of how to do the exercises can be found by going to www.golffitness academy.com and then clicking on "common problems."

■ Government Guidelines

The U.S. government's guidelines for the minimum exercise needed for health recommend thirty minutes of moderate physical activity, in bursts of no less than ten minutes each, on most days. And the recommendation is to start your program with flexibility training before moving to endurance and strength.

■ Flex Time

In golf, strength without flexibility is like locking the genie in the bottle. Flexibility for our purposes is defined as the range of motion of any given joint. Flexible joints use less energy, are more efficient, and are injured less frequently. There is an increased supply of blood to a flexible joint, and the temperature of a healthy joint is higher than that of an unhealthy one, giving it greater elasticity. Flexibility training is also important because it decreases the time it takes for the nerve impulse necessary for muscle contraction to travel from the muscles to the brain and back again, thereby increasing your coordination as well as your reaction time. A flexible muscle is a fast muscle, and that means power.

Studies show that the decline in human flexibility without exercising is about 10 percent per decade, so at age fifty you have lost half of your flexibility. The good news is that this can be slowed dramatically with a regular stretching routine.

The best stretch for golf is also the easiest. You can use it to warm up, to build flexibility, and to learn something about coil, one of the keys to power.

Stand erect with both arms extended fully in front of you. Slide your right arm under your left elbow and hook your right arm around your left until your right palm rests on your right cheek. Now bend your spine until you're in your golf posture and take your backswing, holding the stretch at the top created by your coil for thirty seconds. Then reverse it to stretch the other side of your body.

Competitive Practice: Practice Like You Play

Here's how your brain learns best: First you give it the concept, then you give it the technique, and finally you repeat it over and over until whatever you're practicing becomes part of your blueprint. Its easy for your brain once you've set up the sequence (concept, technique, execution), assuming, of course, that you'll just let it happen. Here is the rule of thumb for your practice: When you're working on a piece of your swing, don't have a specific target; when you're working on hitting the ball to a target, eliminate your focus on swing mechanics.

I teach my students to set aside time for two very different kinds of practice: fundamental practice and practice-like-you-play. You should spend just enough time on fundamental practice to either keep your swing in top form or, if it's slipped a bit, to make the swing adjustment you need to return to top form. Studies show that about 64 percent of all shots taken in a round of golf are from 100 yards and in, so it makes sense that a high percentage of your practice time should be spent putting, chipping, pitching, and in the bunker. Of course, the percentage of time should vary according to your specific needs as shown in your strength/weakness profile.

In general here's what I recommend: Unless you're a beginner who's learning the swing from scratch, spend no more than 20 percent of your practice time working on long game and 50 percent on your short game, for a total of 70 percent. The other 30 percent of the time, practice like you play, because your goal *is not to develop a skill that works on the practice range—it's to develop a skill that works on the golf course.* And here's where your power to imagine comes in. You can actually play a round of golf right there on the practice range, using your imagination to lay out the course, going through your preshot routine, and hitting the shots required given the situation you have created.

Avoid bringing just one or two clubs when you're practicing as you play. Place your bag next to your practice station with all your clubs. The imaginary hole you're playing should have a specific yardage; it might be an actual hole you've played, one you've seen or heard about. Or its outline could be purely your own creation. Select your shot, go through your routine, then execute. Do this until you knock it onto the imaginary green, then give yourself two putts and go to the "next tee."

Working the Ball

To be a complete player you should know how to control the trajectory of your ball as well as draw and fade it (it's called working the ball). But even if you're not at this level yet, understanding what causes your ball to spin left and right, stay low or fly high, will make you a better player because it helps you understand what's happening in your swing when your ball flight takes on these characteristics.

■ *The Draw—It's the Opposite for the Fade*

Before you set your body in position, aim your club face at the target, *and* once your club face is in position, keep it there while you make sure your shoulders, hips, and feet are slightly closed to target. Next, align your body parallel to the line of start, that is, the direction your ball will begin its flight. Because you've pulled your right foot back, adjust your ball position by moving it forward about one ball width in your stance. At this point your club face points where you want your ball to finish (the target) and your body points in the direction you want the ball to start (line of start). From this setup,

The photos show how the setup differs for the draw (a) and the fade (b). To draw the ball, all you have to do is to set up correctly, then take the club away along your foot line and let geometry do its job.

if you make your normal swing along your shoulder line, your club face will be slightly closed at impact, causing a soft draw that curves from right to left back to the target. Your finish reflects a fully released club head with your club head pointing left of the target.

Squeezing the club too tightly will prevent the release of your forearms and wrists, so for the draw, lighten up on your left-hand pressure at address and leave it that way throughout your swing.

The key to curving the ball is to take care of your *direction* at address, then concentrate on producing the correct *distance* with your swing. *Never try to produce direction with your swing.* The shot maker has the correct geometry at address and then allows that geometry to work by simply swinging down the line of start rather than the target line with just enough force to send the ball spinning to target. To produce the right-to-left curve of the draw shot, you'll have to deliver an aggressive blow where the toe is rotating over the heel of your club head. Note that it's not done by flipping your wrists at the ball but by allowing the momentum of your club head to rotate your forearms, pulling the right over the left through impact. The characteristic marking of the draw swing is in the finish, with the back of your right hand looking at the sky and the club head tilted to the left of the target.

Time IQ: Perform a Hit-ectomy

If you listen carefully to thousands of golfers talk about the golf swing as I have over the years, it boils down to this: The majority of golfers view the game of golf as a stick-hit-ball game, with their golf club as the "hitting" instrument. Is that why they call it a "club"?

Please remember that *your golf game will be no better than your concept of what a good golf game should be,* so if you view the club as a hitting instrument, separate and distinct from you, then you are doomed to overmanipulate your golf club. When you see a golfer lunging and lurching, flicking and flinging, what you are actually seeing is the playing out of the concept "stick-hit-ball." The execution of the concept is perfect, but the golf is lousy. You need to take the hit out of your swing—you need a hit-ectomy.

Think of golf as a target game, much like darts. You don't think about the dart or how your arm moves as you throw it. The dart becomes part of you as you play the game. So why not make the club part of you as you play golf? Hit the ball with your swing *motion,* not your club.

Start thinking of your golf club as a temporary prosthesis, a perfectly fitted member that is simply an extension of you the golfer. This way you can make a golf swing that is smooth and flowing, a back-and-forth motion of the arms coupled with a rotation of your body that is uninterrupted by the hit instinct.

Here's a way to get the feeling of the club as part of you. Fasten your five-iron to your left forearm just above your wrist. Use some string or a handkerchief and tie it tightly enough so you get the feeling that the club is an extension of your arm—where it goes, your club follows. You don't have to take a full swing to give your brain the all-important concept that the club swings as part of you, so tee up an eight-iron and hit some very short shots to a definite target only 10 to 20 yards away. Just make half swings with your arms (no wrist cock). After awhile it will become clear that you can strike the ball very solidly and send it to the target without having to "hit" at the ball with the club.

About the Author

T. J. Tomasi, Ph.D., is a Class A PGA Teaching Professional. With a doctorate in education, specializing in learning theory, Tomasi co-founded the LAWs of Golf learning model and has become one of the most respected golf teachers in the nation.

Tomasi is one of the most published golf instructors in the world. His golf page, *Insider Golf,* syndicated by Universal Press Syndicate, appears in over one hundred newspapers and Web sites. He has been featured in a CNN instructional series appearing in flight, in airports, and on CNN. Tomasi was also chosen one of America's Top 100 Teachers by *Golf* magazine and one of the Best Teachers in Florida by *Golf Digest* magazine. A frequent guest speaker at PGA, LPGA, and corporate seminars and workshops, he has also been featured in the highly acclaimed videotape series, *The LAWs of Golf.* He has been head golf professional at three golf clubs and has given over fifty thousand private and group lessons. In addition he was the Sun Country PGA Long Drive Champion and is chair of *Golf* magazine's Science and Golf Research Committee.

Tomasi conducts corporate golf clinics and Maximum Performance Experiences for corporate clients such as Merrill Lynch, Nuveen, Pioneer, and Alliance.

Contact Information
(860) 828-5806
E-mail: pblion@aol.com
Visit the Web site at www.tjtomasi.net

About the Insider Golf *Page*

In April 1999, T. J. Tomasi began authorship of *Insider Golf,* a weekly golf page designed with the golfer in mind, and, just like this book, it is rooted in all aspects of a game loved by millions. The page is published by Universal Press Syndicate, the largest independent newspaper syndicate in the world and the name behind such stars as syndicated columnists Dear Abby and William Buckley, and newspaper page and Internet sensations such as *The Motley Fool* and *NASCAR.* While the exact numbers vary, *Insider Golf* currently appears in over one hundred newspapers across the country and on a host of Web sites.

Andrews McMeel Publishing, the publisher of this book and part of Andrews McMeel Universal, is a leader in book publishing. Each year, the company publishes the work of more than 125 syndicate creators and writers, more than three hundred books, and a prestigious line of calendars and gift and stationery items.